Jan Kott

THE MEMORY OF THE BODY

Essays on Theater and Death

NORTHWESTERN UNIVERSITY PRESS
EVANSTON, ILLINOIS

Northwestern University Press
Evanston, Illinois 60201

Printed in the United States of America

ISBN: 0-8101-1019-9 (cloth)
       0-8101-1043-1 (paper)

Library of Congress Cataloging-in-Publication Data

Kott, Jan.
    The memory of the body : essays on theatre and death / Jan Kott ;
[with translations by Jadwiga Kosicka, Lillian Vallee, and others]
        p.   cm.
    Translated from the Polish.
    ISBN 0-8101-1019-9 (alk. paper); 0-8101-1043-1 (pbk.)
    1. Kott, Jan.
    PN2859.P66K655   1992   91-33302
    891.8'547—dc20   CIP

The paper used in this publication meets the minimum requirements of
American National Standard for Information Sciences—Permanence of Paper
for Printed Library Materials, ANSI Z39.48-1984

THE MEMORY OF THE BODY

Je n'écris pas sur moi, j'écris avec moi-même.

Contents

PART II

PART III

Acknowledgments

My special and warm thanks are due to Jadwiga Kosicka, who not only translated a great part of this book but carefully edited all the other essays and suggested with her infinite patience a lot of corrections.

I also thank the other translators who contributed to this collection: Lillian Vallee ("The Voice of Cassandra," "The Memory of the Body"); Bolesław Taborski ("A Short Treatise on Eroticism," "Aloe," "A Short Treatise on Dying"); Mark Rosenzweig ("The Sexual Triangle"); and Michael and Tara Kott ("The Heart Attack").

The essays collected in *The Memory of the Body* were revised from the following original publications and are used here with permission:

"The Dramaturge" from *New Theatre Quarterly*

"A Lesson in Directing" from *Theater Three*

"Simulators" from *Theater Three*

"The Voice of Cassandra: On Stempowski" from *Formations*

"Kantor's Kaddish" from *Theater Three*

"Kantor, Memory, Mémoire" from *New Theatre Quarterly*

"Grotowski, or The Limit" from *New Theatre Quarterly*

"A Short Treatise on Eroticism," "Aloe," and "A Short Treatise on Dying" from *Polish Writing Today* (Penguin, 1967)

"The Sexual Triangle" from *Partisan Review*

"In the Kitchen of a Shamaness" from *Theater Three*

"The Heart Attack" from *On Signs* (Johns Hopkins University Press, 1985)

"The Memory of the Body" from *Formations*

PART I

THE DRAMATURGE

For Erwin Axer

Eight or nine years ago (or was it perhaps ten?) I was the dramaturge at the B. for more than six months. At one point it had been one of the finest theaters in all of Europe, graced with an imperial box, but its splendor had ended even before World War I. Since then the imperial box has been used occasionally by the chancellor of the Republic, and two or three times in the last fifty years first by the king of Italy and then by either a Belgian or a Dutch queen. All that remains of its former magnificence is the grand marble stairway two stories high which leads to a series of enormous rooms resembling exhibition halls in a museum, their walls covered with huge gilt-framed portraits of actors and actresses going back to the eighteenth century. The earliest pictures show the women in crinolines even in the roles of Desdemona or Portia, and the men in splendid, gold-braided frock coats.

My knowledge of the German language was limited to a few words. Perhaps that is why (although the imperial box was opened especially for me in my capacity as chief dramaturge) what I remember best about that half year's stay is not the actual theatrical performances but the intermissions. Even during the most dramatic moments the performances themselves

3

seemed to me to be little more than a slow-motion animation of the portrait gallery I have just described. But the intermissions were truly spectacular. The B. was one of the few theaters in the world where audiences still appeared in evening clothes (especially in the boxes and first two rows). The ladies came in long dresses, and often during carnival in ball gowns with fur pelisses thrown over their bare shoulders; the gentlemen wore tuxedos and in the back rows stiffly starched shirtfronts and even wing collars of the kind I remember seeing in photographs of my grandfather. An intermission would sometimes last up to an hour, and frequently there would be two such intermissions in a single evening's performance. In the theater's two buffets one could get champagne and tiny canapés with either red lumps of caviar or equally red strips of salmon. The spectators seemed to me to be the evening's leading actors as they slowly walked up to the buffets or looked at their reflections in enormous mirrors.

The administrative offices were housed in the three wings of the theater building, which reminded me of Cracow's Słowacki Theater and even more of the Lvov theater, designed by the same architect or at least according to the same model. The management was located in the main wing. In the side wing with separate stairs were the archives and offices of the lesser dramaturges. There were seven of them, if I remember correctly, and although much younger than I was, they were all bald except for one who had long hair. He was the only one who spoke English. I asked him what all of them did. "What do you mean!" he replied, taken aback by the naïveté of my question, explaining that they read all the plays sent to the theater and summarized them for the Grand Intendant.

My office as the chief dramaturge was located in a separate wing with a separate flight of stairs. The word office is far too modest to describe it. A padded door (intended, no doubt, to protect the dramaturge's secrets from spreading to the outside) led from an anteroom to an apartment complete with a bath-room and a kitchen. There was a cupboard with a china service for four, a supply of coffee, tea, and even a bottle of cognac. The study was furnished with four club chairs, two sofas, and a huge desk with two telephones, one black, one white. The white one was dead and always disconnected, and nobody ever called me on the black one except my wife. And that happened rarely.

And nobody ever visited me there either except the care-taker, who punctually at 11:35 would bring me the daily news-papers, and on Mondays the illustrated weeklies. Of course, all in German. I put them in a pile in the corner, and since no one came and took them away it soon grew into quite a mound.

After two or three weeks of my stay, somewhat uneasy that no one ever asked me to do anything, I made an appointment to see the manager. His office was at least twice as big as mine. And on his desk there were three telephones: a white one, a black one, and a gold one. The gold one, it turned out, was only for decoration. The manager spoke English none too flu-ently and had even greater difficulty understanding my han-dling of the English language. But he was very nice. After hav-ing four rounds of cognac we went to the theater café located on the same square and had some delicious hot dogs with horseradish. The result of this visit was that from then on I re-ceived the *Neue freie Presse* at 10 every morning and on Mon-days twice as many weeklies. But still nobody ever asked me to do anything.

In this fashion the first two months went by. I had grown accustomed to my office and to the silent telephones, and, slightly altering my schedule, I would now show up around noon, drink a glass of cognac, and go all by myself to the café for hot dogs with horseradish. And then one day, at the end of my second month, a girl from the nearby flower shop knocked on the door. She was delivering a bouquet of roses. But they were not for me. They were for Z. His name was familiar to me. Not so long ago he had been considered one of the outstanding theater critics. And he had written a book on Shakespeare as well. To my astonishment it turned out that he had an office in the same entryway but one floor higher.

The next day I paid him a visit. He was aware of my existence and was genuinely glad to see me. "I was the chief dramaturge before you," he said. "My office was one flight down, but now they put me up here. You can see, it's twice as small as yours." It really was smaller, but not as much as he said. "For the past seven months no one has come to see me, and no one has called me either." He pointed to the telephone covered with dust half an inch thick. "And no one could have reached me for that matter because it's disconnected. I get the newspapers only once a week and they are usually a month old. My coffee jars are empty. At least I still get my monthly salary, exactly half of what it used to be. . . . "

Shortly before the end of my stay, I paid my neighbor on the floor above a final visit. "Did you ever hear of N?" he asked. I said of course I had. In the late twenties N. wrote a book on Shakespeare that is still cited in various anthologies. He has been compared to Karl Kraus, and his theater reviews were famous for their wit and venom. "He was the chief dramaturge here too, some time before my appointment. And he still has an office on the third floor."

We went up together. The office turned out to be a small room practically in the attic, with huge piles of newspapers reaching up to the ceiling in all the corners. N. was sitting in a big leather armchair. With his long white beard he resembled a goblin. "I can't remember the last time anyone came up to see me," he said. "I can't even offer you a cup of coffee, because they haven't sent me any for over a year now. And I suspect that the newspapers come from the trash can," the goblin continued, pointing to the piles that were higher than he was by a head. "Even the telephone has been taken away, but it had been out of order for more than a year anyhow. But I still get my monthly salary, a quarter of what the chief dramaturge gets. But you can see for yourselves that everything's going from bad to worse. . . ." And he sunk even deeper in his worn-out leather armchair, almost disappearing from view.

Last May Erwin Axer and I were invited by the same theater to attend a meeting in Berlin with young actors and directors. After a wine reception a lengthy discussion took place. Axer was the last to speak: "For years I've been teaching acting and I know it can be taught. For years I've been teaching directing and I know it can be taught with some pain." "And how to be a dramaturge, can you teach that?" someone asked. "But just what is a dramaturge?" Erwin countered. Then he smiled and pointed at me. "Jan is the one to tell you something about that."

Translated by Jadwiga Kosicka

A LESSON IN
DIRECTING

I t was in the late spring of 1964, or perhaps 1965. At any
rate it was sometime after the English edition of *Shakespeare Our Contemporary* had first appeared. I received a letter from the British Council in Warsaw inviting me to visit
England for two or three months. And there was something in
the letter about British "Shakespearean scholars" looking forward to meeting me. And who did I want to see? I was pleased
to get the invitation, but at the same time I had an uncomforta-
ble feeling that I might be in an awkward position. At the time
I was able to read Shakespeare in English after a fashion, but
only if I had a Polish translation alongside that I could consult.
And often more than one. As for my ability to speak the language, sometimes I managed well enough, but the results were
quite unpredictable. For instance, at one point I had to greet a
delegation from the British Foreign Ministry visiting Warsaw
University. I greeted them, "Welcome to the Ministry of
Strange Affairs." "Strange" was my impromptu translation
from the French *étranger*. The Britishers loved it.

L. told me to accept the invitation and go to school in England. The idea was splendid, but I felt ill at ease introducing myself to a gentleman from the British Council as if I were the hero of Gombrowicz's *Ferdydurke*. Fortunately he had a wonderful sense of humor, just like those British diplomats from the "Strange Ministry." Delighted, he enrolled me in a two-month English-language course at Oxford.

It wasn't just that I was the oldest student in that summer school. Except for a couple of boys, the participants in the course were young Swedish and Norwegian girls. All blonde and long legged. But it wasn't their long legs that mattered, but the fact that although they had come to the school, they already spoke English well. From the very first week, I was the worst student in the class. I would invariably get a great big "F" on every dictation. In Polish we call such a low grade a "two" or maybe it's even a "zero." To make things worse, when I invited one of the Swedish girls for a boat ride, I fell in the water as I was gazing at the greenery along the shore.

It was sometime in the third week of the course when I received a letter from Tom Fleming at the Lyceum Theatre in Edinburgh. Besides telling me that he was coming to Oxford to see me, he asked me to direct two of Mrożek's plays at his theater in the very immediate future. All expenses were to be covered plus an honorarium in British pounds that was very generous given the rate of exchange into Polish zlotys. I was destined to keep on playing Ferdydurke it seemed. I was delighted. But there was a hitch—I had never directed before in my life. So before Fleming's visit to Oxford I went to London to see Peter Brook. "Just how do you do it?" I asked him. Peter took my question very seriously. "There are only two great secrets to directing which you must never forget. During the rehearsals as you're looking at the stage from the fifth or the seventh row, you must instruct your actors never to block each other. And if two actors are to come through the same door, you must tell them which one is to enter first and which second, otherwise they'll bump into one another. All the rest of it is of no importance and won't give you any trouble whatsoever."

And, actually, the rest of it gave me no trouble whatsoever. The actors were professionals, several quite extraordinary. My assistant was also highly professional despite her young age. The useful thing I learned from her was to avoid saying, "Yes, yes, yes" and "No, no, no." "Jan," she explained, "once is enough!" The Mrożek's plays that I directed were *The Police* and *Out at Sea*. I was full of ideas. It seemed to me that *The Police* was too static and then I didn't know what to do with the actors. Luckily the set designer was quite ingenious. I asked him to construct on the stage a kind of "bowling alley" made of planks along which a heavy ball could be bowled to knock over the wooden pins at the other end. Thus the actors were busy bowling. At the moment of greatest tension, when all the characters had finally arrested each other, the pins at the far end stopped falling over. As for *Out at Sea,* I had no trouble at all. The actor playing the role of Fat was the spitting image of Churchill, and when he proposed that they eat Thin first, the audience burst into peals of laughter. I felt sure that Mrożek would have been pleased. I think it was the first English production of these plays.

The rehearsals lasted three weeks, and there was a party after the last performance. The actors presented me with a gift: a wonderful camel's hair sweater. I wore it for many years. As we said good-bye, I told them that there are three separate languages: English, Scottish, and Kottish. They had no doubts whatsoever that that was the case.

I managed to return to Oxford just in time for the graduation ceremony. To my astonishment, besides a certificate with the highest grades, I received a bouquet of flowers and a citation of merit saying that the school was proud to have among its students the great Polish Shakespearean scholar. Afterward the director of the school invited me to come have a glass of sherry with him. We bumped into each other in the doorway.

After returning to Poland Lidia used to say, "I sent my husband to school but he ran away and joined a theater."

Translated by Jadwiga Kosicka

SIMULATORS

I did my military service in Zambrów. That was a couple of years before World War II, now, hard as it is to believe, more than fifty years ago. Zambrów had always been a dreary little town, but that cold, rainy autumn it was even drearier than usual. Even its main street, with its two bars and a church, had turned into a huge gutter, and the open fields surrounding the town were transformed into a vast soggy marsh. We had to crawl through the mud for hours on end. No one in our group was spared. Picked up a year or two earlier at a Communist street rally, I had my papers marked "ps" (politically suspect); so did many of my friends, mainly Ukrainians and Jews. Our division received "penal" training with extra harsh discipline. The only hope was to end up in the hospital. And best of all would be in the Warsaw military hospital. But simulation was by no means safe or easy. Checking in for morning sick call at the infirmary without a fever was risky once; the second time you went straight to the brig. But in the army as in life, anything you want can be achieved through patience and perseverance. In no time I mastered the art of "self-induced" fever. All it takes is to tap the thermometer lightly when it's placed under your arm. The only catch is not to overdo the tapping—the mercury will shoot up and the simulation will be promptly unmasked.

For a good two weeks I stubbornly tapped away at the thermometer. Twice I was caught and sent to the brig. But I kept on tapping. And finally I was sent to the military hospital in Warsaw, a beautiful hospital located near the Łazienki Park. But there they stuck the thermometers in the patients' mouths. I thought I was finished. But the thermometer showed 98.8. By the evening it rose to 100. The next morning I was X-rayed. I had shadows on my left lung and infiltration on my right. It turned out that I was too good a simulator. Thus I had "over-simulated" a true illness.

Daniel C. Gerould in his excellent and intellectually stimulating essay "Imaginary Invalids: A Theatre of Simulated Patients" (*Yale/Drama*, 1988) writes about the interactions and fragile dividing line between acting and simulation. There is a professional group of actors in New Jersey called the Simulators. The group simulates ailments before large audiences at seminars and conferences for medical students, practicing physicians, and real patients. The genuinely sick person—as Gerould aptly points out—is not a good patient. He needlessly arouses his doctor's compassion, mixes up his symptoms, has pains where he shouldn't have them, wants to be too sick or not sick enough. To simulate an illness, one must be healthy. The actors of that professional company diligently research and study the symptoms of diseases, not unlike simulators in the army and in prisons. They are the exemplary, the model sick, the ideal patients that doctors and pharmacists are looking for. After all, what counts for them is the right diagnosis, and perhaps even more the right prescription.

But whom is the actor playing? The sick person? No, the truly sick person is not a model patient. The actor plays not the sick person but the perfect simulator. Or more precisely: the actor plays a healthy individual who has learned his illness by heart, like a role. Here the sickness is the role, not the sick person. If *everyone* is a soul-in-bodied/embodied, then the actor plays the *Other*, and this Other is also a soul-in-bodied. But the actor has only his own body, and all he can offer that other soul-in-bodied/embodied is another soul. There are two souls in acting, often more than two, but there is only one body. Therefore simulation in our soul-in-bodied is an imitation/assumption of another body. In acting we are many: in simulation we are divided. In acting one body has many souls; in simulation the soul has various bodies.

But in madness, real or feigned, played or simulated, the differences may appear blurred. Hamlet simulates madness. The actor plays not a mad Hamlet, but a Hamlet feigning madness. But Hamlet simulates madness so skillfully that he may have been genuinely affected by that "antique disposition" (1.5.172). Freud showed that Hamlet himself does not know the cause of his own neurosis. He subconsciously avoids killing Claudius, since Claudius took on the role of this new Oedipus in killing his father. A very bold argument, but even if a director believes it, how is the actor to play such a Hamlet? This Hamlet simulates madness without knowing that he is afflicted with it. Who then is playing whom, and who is simulating whom?

Gerould also mentions the shows at the Salpêtrière asylum in Paris put on by the famous Dr. Charcot for his guests, among them writers, actors, and actresses such as Sarah Bernhardt. These shows had actors both on the stage and in the audience. But on the stage Dr. Charcot's patients were featured; the mad played the mad in these shows. Dr. Charcot was by no means the first to put on a theater of the mad. In Shakespeare's day, in the Restoration and long after, large crowds used to flock to Bedlam, a hospital for the insane located in the suburbs of London, where they could watch madmen specially rounded up for the occasion. The action in a number of plays of the period takes place in the presence of the mentally deranged.

Freud was a pupil of Charcot and attended these shows. Indisputably, Freud's early works on hysteria, so seminal for the emergence of his theory of the subconscious, can be traced back to these experiences. Hysteria is an affliction of the soul, not of the body. All symptoms, even the most physiological, most corporeal, such as lack of menstruation or, on the contrary, prolonged bleeding, impotence, all kinds of aches and pains, sometimes even stigmata, have their origin in long-suppressed traumas. It is the sick soul that requires treatment, not the body. In this case the soul turns out to be an unconscious but consummate simulator/manipulator. Like a prisoner who wants to get out of his cell at any price, the soul keeps torturing its own body in order to be cured. Or perhaps to torment itself.

A woman who has failed to have an orgasm simulates it. A woman who has had an orgasm simulates frigidity. In both cases the woman deceives her partner. But if she deceives herself . . . who then is deceiving whom? Is the body deceiving the soul, or the soul the body? ("The tongue belies all sound, and sound all thought," Adam Mickiewicz, *Forefathers' Eve*, Part III). In the crudest simulation and in the greatest acting we are deceiving the other with our own body, but in the profoundest self-simulation, as in self-abuse, the deceived and the deceiver are one and the same person. Sartre coined a term for it: "bad faith" (*mauvaise foi*), but my terms are more lucid. And more useful in the analysis of acting.

Once in Stratford-upon-Avon—that was years ago too—after attending a Shakespearean production, I found myself in a pub, a well-known gathering place for actors. Judging by the number of toasts proposed, it must have been someone's birthday or a theater anniversary of some kind. John Gielgud recognized me and invited me to his table. It was his turn to propose a toast. "In Kean's time," Gielgud began, "the king's brother had a lot of trouble with his daughter. Desirous of novelty, she would sleep every night with a different man. That caused a great deal of embarassment to the whole family. One day, the father of the insatiable creature made Kean a proposal. 'Every evening you are someone else: a king's son or his clown, a Moor or a Milanese nobleman, a master and his servant, a judge and a robber. So I pray you to go to my daughter after each performance, without taking off the costume . . .' And that is what happened. For the next six months the great Kean spent every other night with the king's brother's daughter. After Kean's first visit she stopped looking for a new man. After six months the king's brother summoned Kean again. 'Our daughter is happy with you. We are going to bestow the title of Sir upon you. Take her for your wife.' 'I cannot,' was Kean's answer. 'And just why not?' said the astonished brother of the king of England. 'I am impotent,' the great Kean replied."

Sir John (I don't remember whether he had already been knighted then) raised his mug filled with the heavy dark Irish beer called Guinness and said: "Glory to the art of acting."

In his essay Gerould also discusses Molière's *Imaginary Invalid*. Argan simulates illnesses. All kinds of illnesses. His family and his doctors assist him in his feigning: the doctors because every sick person increases their income; the family in the hope that Argan will carry the simulation to its conclusion and die. And that is what happened. But it was not Argan who died on stage but Molière. The mortally sick author was stricken while playing the role of the imaginary invalid. Gerould is right. Only the healthy can play the sick. Molière played his last role very badly indeed. The imaginary invalid died.

Translated by Jadwiga Kosicka

THE VOICE OF CASSANDRA

On Stempowski

He would sit for hours on a stump in the middle of the flower bed. The brush beneath him was thick with ivy and periwinkle, and the azalea bushes grew up in palisades around him. The tree stump protruded high above the plantings and made an excellent lookout. He reminded me of the watchman in Aeschylus's prologue to *Agamemnon* who from the roof of the palace of Atreus patiently awaits signs that the war is over. I poured nuts and pumpkin seeds in his direction but he would never come close. He was incorruptible. Finding food did not appear to be his preoccupation, since he spent whole hours on the tree stump. He must have had other concerns.

The chipmunk is unknown in Poland. It is a small squirrel with a short tail and a gray zigzag down its back. He has numerous enemies. Last summer the neighbor's black cat began to frequent our garden; she fawned on me but had her eye on the chipmunk. He disappeared shortly thereafter. Every once in a while I come across him on the other side of the road as he darts in and out of the underbrush. Less and less frequently.

Stempowski taught me to read, write, and distrust. Learning to write came easiest, learning to read took many years, and learning to distrust began only when Stempowski's voice was so faint that I could barely hear him. In the book *From Berdyczów to Rome* there is a story, "The Smugglers' Library," about his stay in the Carpathian Mountains at the Hungarian border during the last months of the war. I first heard the story when we met after the war in the Café du Théâtre in Bern, on Kramgasse next to the old clock where Russian émigrés got together before World War I. This story of how smugglers were suddenly transformed into librarians must have had particular significance for Stempowski because he returned to it over and over again. It was a philosophical tale like the one about flying carpets: The books people carry in sacks flung over their shoulders or take with them on long and risky expeditions have magic powers. Left behind in mountain shelters or forest inns by murdered wanderers or those who had to flee, they await new readers who will one day need them as desperately as tobacco and bread.

As early as the mid-thirties, Stempowski had a consciousness of Western civilization's coming to an end. His catastrophism was different from that of the poets, less apocalyptic, not intoxicating itself with visions of destruction and not seeking either moral vindication or intellectual justification. This was, I am searching for the right word, a defensive catastrophism. Stempowski observed the symptoms and mechanisms of the approaching catastrophe coolly and alertly, but for him the most important thing was to rescue what could still be saved. He knew that civilizations are frail and subject to destruction, but he also knew that no civilization vanishes without a trace. Civilizations leave behind species of trees (he wrote about the trees of Bern tenderly and with expertise in his French book) and methods for cultivating the soil; the very essence of their history remains in their trade routes—

along which people travel centuries afterward—and in the graves and ruins of settlements located exactly where new ones spring up. This essence of history is contained in the few books that have survived.

I remember how Stempowski said, long before the September of 1939, that people should select very carefully one or two hundred of the most important books and that they should hide them even more carefully. Soon there would come a time, he predicted, when librarians would have to transform themselves into smugglers. He included in his list of important books Daniel Defoe's *Journal of the Plague Year* and Thucydides— because of his description of the plague that preceded the fall of Athens. The plague was for him the paradigm of a mortal enemy that has slipped within the city walls as the gates are locked. It is too late to leave the city, all moral and customary norms are shattered, and choices seem, to all appearances, to be senseless. What, asked Stempowski, ought one do in a city in which the plague runs rampant?

Machiavelli's *The Prince* also belonged on Stempowski's list. For him, the absolute ruler was the same as the deadly plague. In this Renaissance handbook of efficient terror he tried to find an explanation for the acts of the contemporary prince that seemed aimless and irrational, such as Piłsudski's ostentatious contempt for the Sejm or Hitler's spectacular burning of the Reichstag. The ruler who gains power legally or semi-legally, in order to show that he is the prince, must stand above law, morality, and custom. To have the Senate confirm your godhead, you must turn a horse into a senator. Open violence and unconcealed contempt are the coronation and investiture of the dictator.

I did not remember our conversations about Shakespeare and discovered only years later that Stempowski also taught me how to read Shakespeare as our contemporary. My master wrote in one of his early essays:

> It seems to me that as a measure of times such as our own,
> Shakespeare's philosophy, a tragic philosophy such as that
> in *Troilus and Cressida* might be more accurate: the world
> of the protagonists is lost; everything that is the greatness
> and hope of others is lost; only the wretched and vile re-
> mains. I think that this is the most beautiful and appropri-
> ate reading we have, profoundly real, bringing us close to
> tragic reality and removing us from that whole wretched
> half-world which Europe has become. I read *Troilus* with
> my students and I was horrified by Shakespeare's rele-
> vance, his artistic and philosophical relevance.

Before the war, Stempowski compared the general situation
in Europe to a besieged town or fortified camp. In a town
under siege the people are forced to make a choice: ourselves or
the enemy. The story in a fortified camp justifies both the cur-
tailing of power as well as mass executions. If we do not murder you, they will murder us. Sometimes one can even use this
arrangement to convince the victims. As one of the communi-
qués from American Army headquarters in Vietnam: "The city
was destroyed in order to save it." The West, wrote Stempowski, imposed the choice between Hitler and Stalin on Eastern
Europe.

In a town overrun by the plague, in a fortified camp, and in
occupied zones the choices are always limited, but probably it is
not a wise thing to believe the newspapers, to announce your
arrival, or to ask gendarmes the way. In these extreme circum-
stances, from which, as Stempowski used to say, "let the Good
Lord forbid," the prognoses of professional intellects are a dis-
appointment and one should believe instead the experience of
those social groups that, for centuries distrustful of all authori-
ties, are accustomed to relying on their own wisdom as well as
tried and true practices. "For the longest time," Stempowski
wrote in a letter in March 1942, "the true intellects, wise men,
and visionaries have been highlanders and rabbis, and by no

means the imposters who lawlessly exploit these titles and who are always ready to write books about burning in ovens, lost forever in ignorance and wantonness. Unfortunately, the western part of the continent no longer has either highlanders or rabbis."

Stempowski would have a good laugh if he knew that the civilization of Orthodox Jewry and Carpathian highlanders was being called a "subculture" by "ignorant intellectuals." These Jews and highlanders saw—in their formal and rigorous rules, customs, and rituals for birth, marriage, and death, as well as the purchase or selling of a horse, in the distinction between "clean" and "unclean," and the avoidance of "evil"—the passing on from generation to generation of universal and important experiences. When Lévi-Strauss stood to a drumroll under the dome of the French Academy—in a splendidly embroidered dress coat and three-cornered hat, épée at his side—as one of the Academy's new "immortals," he began his speech with the reminder that not many weeks before he had partaken in a similar ceremony on the shores of the Pacific on an Indian reservation in northern Canada. An initiation is a new birth and the candidate, after a period of difficult trials, stood before the society to which he would from that moment on belong, in formal attire covering him from head to foot and with weapons to protect him from evil. Drums, of a different shape, rumbled, just as they did under the Academy's dome, although to a different beat, after which the newly initiated delivered his sermon.

If there are deeply religious people, Stempowski was a man who was, in the same sense, deeply unreligious. He had no faith in doctors, lay or ecclesiastic. He did not believe in, to use Norwid's words, "doctors' offices" or fashionable "apparatuses." He considered collective declarations passed without opposition to be of dubious value, written predictably in the style of an official newspaper or to the rhythm of a Polish folk dance. Instead he listened intently to faraway voices, from all the lands that were taken away. He reflected on the letters of his friends. He believed eyewitnesses and people whose character, farsightedness, and discernment he could trust. Stempowski was probably the first Polish émigré writer who visited Germany after the war and began to carry on a dialogue with the Germans. The journals of his many trips to Germany, Italy, Austria, and Holland were published in *Kultura*. These were neither adventure nor scholarly travels. In Sulmona, the place of the first exile of Ovid, Stempowski began to think of the fate of the author of *Ars amandi*, and of his later lonely death among Sarmatians and Scythians. These were travels made after the deluge, and Stempowski sought people who were ready for the new flood and perhaps had a plan for building a new ark. Of these travel journals the last is the most characteristic, recording his trip to Yugoslavia and his visit to Nikolai Mikhailov, one of the first dissidents arrested, thrown out of the university, deprived of the right to publish or to get a passport to travel abroad. "When saying good-bye to Mikhailov in the port a few days later," Stempowski wrote in his *Journal*, "I had the feeling that I was saying good-bye to an old friend. If not for the difference in age, he could have been a colleague from my Russian gymnasium."

In his *Letters from Bern* one can find the crystallization of the specific posture whose seriousness and value surfaced only after Stempowski's death. There are two differing dissident traditions: the Aryan and the Puritan, the Central or East European and the Anglo-Saxon. But common to all dissident postures is the casting off of the state religion and the recognition that private conscience and the unmuddled light of the mind are the ultimate judge that allows one to distinguish law from legalized lawlessness, a just war from an invasive one, obedience from slavery. In recent years not just these general premises of a dissident's posture have become relevant again. The most unexpected and thought-provoking characteristic of the early dissident movement is its revival of long-forgotten, old-fashioned, almost cottage-industry forms of protest and resistance: samizdat, the personal channels of passing information, silent pickets, individual hunger strikes, books smuggled abroad, letters signed by a select group. I belong to the war generation that believed in the mass character of a political movement in which discipline and obedience seemed to be the only effective means of changing the world. The experiences of recent times have shown that the great police systems, just like the most modern planes and computers, have their weak spots. Entire armies of policemen and informers must work hard to interfere with the meeting of merely ten people who have determined to speak their minds. In this world, which reminds one more and more of a slab of pork fat cut into two pieces with a dull knife, the quiet voice of the dissident cottage industry has been impossible to jam. The dissident posture has shown not only its moral values but also its political efficacy. This is one of the few feeble hopes that have remained. And dissidents are not just in countries dominated by the Communist party.

"Monsieur Homais the Marxist," wrote one of my Polish friends from Paris not long ago, "is something rather difficult for us to stomach." Equally hard to stomach is Monsieur Homais the Freudian, and I confess that, with all due respect to semiotics, this pharmacist from Flaubert in his new role as a poststructuralist does not excite me. The indifferent and elegant sophistry of the latest Parisian and Yale mandarins is finally just one more symptom of moral indifference. The great centers of Western civilization have undergone far more serious transformations, which appear irreversible.

Leicester Square and the streets surrounding it east of Soho have long been a neighborhood half-residential, half-devoted to entertainment. Recently, after not having been in London for several years, I turned into one of the side streets a few feet from Leicester Square and suddenly found myself in a

Chinatown. This was not a tourist attraction and shared nothing with the Chinatowns of New York or San Francisco. I asked directions in English but no one understood. In tiny restaurants the menu was given only in Chinese. In the shop windows there were strange dried fish, plucked birds hanging head down, black hunks of smoked meat similar to fried rats suspended from hooks. I knew these shop windows from the small provincial towns I had visited during my travels in China. But the provincial Chinese town lost in great expanses of Asia I now found in the very center of London.

Returning home one night in Paris, I suddenly saw on the empty place de Saint Sulpice a pair of Japanese women in elaborately embroidered kimonos mincing along with tiny steps like two splendid white peacocks. The great international hotels are almost exclusively occupied by Japanese tourist groups. In first-rate hotels one meets no one but Arabs; just as all the luxury clinics have been bought out by the oil sheiks. For the last few years the great houses of fashion have, in their winter and summer collections, been showing first high Circassian fur caps and wide pants tucked into boots, then Chinese jackets buttoned to the neck, colored kimonos, and silk pants; next came white turbans and all kinds of saris; the last collections brought Arab yashmaks and Bedouin burnooses. The great fashion houses are being very consistent in preparing for the end of Europe.

Historians, chroniclers, and travelers wrote that in the Rome of the Caesars in the second and third century, there were practically no Romans and that even Latins found themselves in the minority. Beyond the Tiber, on the great square in front of the Baths of Caracalla, even in the Forum one came across nothing but black Nubians, Huns with protruding cheekbones, or tow-haired giants from the North. It was at this time that a violent orientalization of Roman gods took place. All of this happened a good one hundred years before the invasion by the Vandals and Visigoths and before Alaric entered

Rome. I personally feel no great loss when thinking about the fall of Rome, although the destruction of Troy "which burns eternally" always fills me with helpless despair. The civilization to which we belong was built by people the Romans called barbarians. But I don't know if this or the fact that the building took many centuries is of much comfort.

Stempowski devoted one of his finest essays to Cassandra. Cassandra had the gift of prophecy and the gods did not deprive her of it. But Apollo, with whom she would not sleep or, in another version, whose child she would not bear, punished her in an extremely cruel way. She could prophesy but no one would believe her. No one believes her even now.

The books that Stempowski left behind in the forest inn will have a long wait for a new reader.

Translated by Lillian Vallee

LEC AND HIS APHORISMS

I saw him for the last time several weeks before I left for America. It was at noon in the fashionable cafeteria at the state publishing house, not in the back where the tables are, but right by the entrance where the new publications are displayed on the counter. It was known that he was seriously ill and recently I'd heard that he had had a metastasis. He really did look awful and his clothes were hanging off him. "Look at me," he said, "I'm not a Jew now. I'm half of a Jew."

A few weeks before he had had a sallow complexion, but he wasn't so frightfully thin. That was at the same cafeteria. Lec had brought with him a big envelope with American stamps on it. He pulled out a sizable volume. "Look," he said, "Lec's aphorisms alongside verses from the Bible. There's nothing more to look forward to. Lec and God the Father are cited on facing pages."

"Illiterates have to dictate." Lec once described how he discovered that aphorism. He actually expressed it that way: "discovered." Because the most striking of his sayings often have something of a discovery about them—dis-covery, as though they existed somewhere previously. Lec saw them, but *how* he saw them! "I was at some friends'. In an adjoining room some voices could be heard. I opened the door. There were two little girls in the room. The elder was six. I doubt that the younger was more than four. The younger was dictating a fairy tale in a very loud voice. 'I have to dictate,' she said, 'because I don't know how to write.' " It could be a scene out of a comedy. Lec's aphorisms, even the most unexpected, are scenes from a comedy, fixed for a moment, fixed forever. But a moment later that scene from a comedy of manners is being played on the great stage of politics. "Illiterates have to dictate."

Sometimes in these aphorisms of Lec there is fairy-tale enchantment. But a fairy tale seen from the wrong end. "Open Sesame" are the magic words. They open the door so that one can come in. But what kind of magic words are needed so that one can get out? "Open Sesame! I want to get out." And here's another aphorism from the country where fear reigns. "Don't talk about your dreams. What if the Freudians come to power?"

And here's another aphorism that he saw. Some women were lying on the beach. "Are naked women intelligent?" Maybe they are. But if they aren't, who cares? This aphorism is not intended for feminists. Even if they are intelligent.

Adam Tarn, the editor of the theatrical monthly *Dialog,* was, I think, the first person to realize how thoroughly theatrical Lec's aphorisms are. Not only are they quintessential comedy, they are often an illumination of comedy, of comedy as a genre. "What do you do," asked a friend, "when you find in your own bed your wife's lover with another woman?" Tarn put Lec's aphorisms between the plays that he published. For each of his "Unkempt Thoughts" Lec demanded a peculiar fee. It was the equivalent of a gram of pure gold according to the latest exchange rate on the Vienna market. Lec considered himself a subject of Franz Joseph's Hapsburg Empire and didn't believe in any market except the one in Vienna. He died of cancer a few months after our last conversation in the cafeteria at the state publishing house.

Translated by Lillian Vallee

ON GOMBROWICZ AND SCHULZ

I

I t was not so long ago, and yet there are almost no traces left. Of the buildings that once stood there, not even ruins remain and many of the people who lived in them are dead. Of the house in Małoszyce where Gombrowicz was born, only the green tiles from the ornamental stoves have survived. They are piled up in a shack: "Maybe someone will buy them for a stove to cook potatoes for pigs?" The estate was parceled out among the local peasants at the beginning of the war. Zofia Popek, born in 1907, still remembers the young master very well. Her mother had been the Gombrowiczes' cook. After the war the Popeks bought the manor house with the outbuildings, the park, and the surrounding land. Today Zofia Popek's daughter's house stands exactly where the manor house once stood. The pond in which the Popek children used to swim with the young master has dried up. "So much the better," Popek rejoices. "At last it can be used as a pasture for the cows!'' The park's ancient trees were cut for firewood years ago. "The big rocks that once flanked the park's entrance now lie around in the Popeks' yard and the hens use them as roosts."

These are excerpts from the opening chapter of Joanna Siedlecka's book, *The Young Master of Małoszyce*. Reading this book is like watching a movie. But this Polish movie was directed by History. Of the Gombrowiczes' manor house only the foundations are left, but the local people "know that the Master Witold made it in the world." City folk, both Poles and foreigners, come here in droves and ask endlessly about the writer. "Ladies and Gentlemen, you're looking at the family estate of our great poet, Witold Gombrowicz," the visitors are informed by Zofia Popek's grandson, an engineer from Kielce and self-appointed guide whenever he comes to Małoszyce to see his mother. "This is where he was born and grew up." *Ferdydurke* is being repeated for the umpteenth time, but in this version Witold is playing the bard's role, and I can imagine what a laugh he would have.

At the end of World War II the house in nearby Wsoła where Witold's elder brother lived after he got married was first converted into the local militia headquarters, then briefly used as a silkworm farm, and when the worms all died off, turned into a home for retarded children. In the former guest room, "where Witold used to write, the most severely handicapped children are housed . . . strapped into their beds to keep them from crawling out and hurting themselves. The windows are grated for safety's sake, not to prevent bats from flying in." Gombrowicz was terrified of bats.

Bodzechów, the former estate of the Kotkowski family (Witold's mother was a Kotkowska), where Witold spent a good part of his childhood, is now an agricultural cooperative. Of the palace built in the eighteenth century only the foundations remain. And the " 'female,' as the local people call the goddess Ceres, now toppled to the ground and with its arms chopped off, is the only sculpture left of the many that once adorned the park." It had been undermined by people looking for gold buried under it, and when nothing was found, "they hammered off the head and the arms in the hope of finding the gold inside." In this bitter epitaph on the family saga, the endless history of the Polish estates is repeated as in a bad dream.

On Służewska Street in Warsaw where the Gombrowiczes lived for more than twenty years there are not even any ruins left. Not only is the house gone, so is the street. But the building at 35 Chocimska Street, where Gombrowicz finished *Ferdydurke,* is still standing. After the war the Gombrowiczes' apartment was used as a canteen by the Bureau for the Reconstruction of Warsaw. To this day there is a mark on the floor where the big coffee maker stood.

So much for the buildings. Now let us turn to the family saga. When the war broke out Janusz, the eldest of the brothers, was living on his estate in Potoczek. During one of many robberies he shot and killed a bandit. Or it could have been a partisan. Fearing retribution he fled with his family to Warsaw. After the Warsaw uprising in 1944, he and his son were taken to the German camp at Mauthausen. Three months after his release from the camp he was arrested in Warsaw and sentenced to three years in prison for supposedly killing the partisan. Once out of prison he couldn't find a permanent job. Or perhaps he wasn't looking too hard. Like Witold, Janusz hated any form of dependence. He supported himself by illegal trading in gold and jewelry. He lived the life of a recluse in a one-room apartment in Grochów, a working-class district of Warsaw. He had two shirts, the one on his back, the other soaking in a pail. And like all the Gombrowiczes he was asthmatic. Janusz died in 1968, a year before Witold.

The middle brother, Jerzy, was a lieutenant in the uhlans during the 1920 Polish-Soviet war. He married a rich heiress and Wsoła was part of her dowry. At their wedding reception in Radom roast peacock was served. Jerzy hunted, played cards, and entertained guests. Running his estate did not interest him in the least. He gradually leased the land and kept selling whatever he could sell. Timber and cattle. He used to say that war and revolution were coming soon and everything would go to the devil. He was right. He could have been a character in one of Witkacy's plays. But I am not sure in which one. Maybe in *The Shoemakers*? After the war Jerzy lived in Radom in a two-room apartment with a kitchen. His wife was apparently an excellent cook. Jerzy wrote articles for two regional newspapers, and at mass meetings he spoke in favor of "socialism" and against "the capitalists and landowners." And he kept on inviting guests to play cards and he kept on drinking, even with his former farmhands from Wsoła, who supplied him with homemade cheese, butter, and meat. When he died in 1971 almost the entire village came to his funeral.

Witold's elder sister, Rena, the only ugly duckling in the family, never married. Before the war she worked at the Institute for Blind Children at Laski. After the war she lived with her mother in Kielce in rented one-room apartments. Rena took care of her mother until the latter's death in 1959. She outlived her mother by only two years. Like her brothers Rena was asthmatic. Her applications for a retirement pension were turned down three times.

Józef, Janusz's son, did not return to Poland after his release from Mauthausen. After many years of wandering, he settled in Paris. Józef is the first of the Gombrowiczes to become a blue-collar worker. He married a French woman and they have four children: two daughters and two sons. No one in the family speaks Polish. Such is the last chapter in the family saga.

According to rumor, or perhaps he made up the story himself, in Argentina Gombrowicz conferred a princely title on himself. For a long time I thought that his artistocratic poses were part of the game in his system of "annihilation." An air of condescension or social provocation he much favored: "Mr. Kott, being of a plebeian stock, you can't possibly comprehend this . . ." he once told me. And not until recently did I finally understand how deeply Gombrowicz was rooted in the landed-gentry tradition to which he belonged. This manifested itself not only in his phobias but also in his ridicule of aristocratic snobbery. In order to throw out the ballast, it must be there to start with. As Joanna Siedlecka writes in *The Young Master,* Gombrowicz received Krystyna Zachwatowicz with unusual warmth just because she happened to be a maternal cousin of his. That discovery made them feel "at home."

In 1965 Krystyna and I combed various Parisian flea markets in search of broken armchairs, discarded mattresses, and rickety wardrobes for the sets she was designing for *Ivona,* which Jorge Lavelli staged with much success. Two years earlier Krystyna's sets for the Polish premiere of *The Marriage* featured scraps of metal, wrecked cars, and punctured tires. At the time it was an innovative and stunning concept for stage design. But I dream of seeing the plays of Gombrowicz, and those of Witkacy too, done in costumes from the interwar years and with a painterly vision and background closer to the text and rich in real detail. It seems to me that *The Marriage* demands a setting showing the Kielce or Sandomierz landscape. " 'When I saw *The Marriage* on stage, I felt as if I were at home,' says Mrs. Marchwińska. In the old house, of course. Of the old Bodzechów house that she remembers very little has been left."

The author of *The Young Master* tracked down and interviewed the eighty-year-old Maria Marchwińska, like Witold's mother a Kotkowska. "Marchwińska would recognize in Gombrowicz's works many actual Bodzechów situations, characters, landscapes, and even phrases that she had known. The action of Gombrowicz's thriller, *The Possessed,* takes place in a strange manor house that is a perfect image of the one at

Bodzechów. The Drunkard in *The Marriage* pronounces the crucial word 'finger' in a strange way that Marchwińska calls 'Bodzechów talk.' "

I was never an admirer of the "genetic" or the "psychogenic" interpretation, but Siedlecka's account of Witold's family offers unexpected keys and tropes for understanding Gombrowicz. For example, intermarriage had been practiced in the Kotkowski family for generations. It helped keep their estates intact, but it also produced a number of eccentrics and even some outright madmen. At least two of Witold's aunts and two of his uncles were mentally ill. Recalling his childhood in a conversation with Dominique de Roux, Gombrowicz said, "I inhaled madness." Witold's mother was a thin, reserved, and often totally withdrawn matron who was usually referred to as a "mummy" by the house servants and the peasants. "You say the son of the mummy, I mean the son of Ignacy's daughter, was a writer? Well, well, the old family weakness had to pop out even in him!" That was the reaction of a former farmhand for the Kotkowski family.

In this unpretentious and moving book, which is a relief after so much pompous "scholarly" criticism, the most striking documents are the faithfully recorded conversations with former servants who had worked for the family either on their estates or later in Warsaw. After all the intervening years the former butler Więckowski still remembers how at a formal dinner the young master warned the guests, "Don't eat so much, or you'll choke to death!" And then later, turning to a lady in a white summer dress seated next to him, he asked, "Imagine yourself getting into your carriage and someone spills sorrel soup all over your dress, what would you do?" As he was strolling one day in Saski Garden with some young ladies from a school for girls of good families, Witold treated them to laxative chocolates. The young ladies just barely made it to nearby Piłsudski Square. Character seems unchangeable from childhood on, but in Gombrowicz practical jokes and social life as a form of constant aggression became transformed into a unique Gombrowiczian theater.

Aniela, who worked for the family for over thirty years, now lives in Sokołów. When Siedlecka talked with her, Aniela was already eighty-seven years old, but she remembered everything. Especially Witold. "You dumb, benighted maidservant," he would yell if admonished by Aniela, "show proper respect for your master and benefactor!" But one has to be deaf to miss the tenderness so obvious in this exclamation. In a letter to Aniela from Argentina Gombrowicz wrote: "When I saw the envelope with the name Sokołów on it, I knew it was a letter from you, Aniela, and memory brought back to me Służewska Street and all the fights I had with you and all the 'dumb, benighted servants' I used to call you, jokingly of course, since you were more a friend to us than a servant."

He would listen intently to the inflections of her "Sokołów" dialect and took from her the expression "to my astoundishment." In his relation to the "dumb Aniela" there was something more than enchantment with "inferiority." In a profound sense Gombrowicz's relation to Aniela, with whom he used to talk about himself, about life, about people, is reminiscent of Proust's relationship with his housekeeper, Céleste. "Aniela is the most intelligent person in this house," he said over and over again. And she was certainly the only person in the house to whom he would read aloud what he had written. As was the case with Proust. "*Ferdydurke* is very famous," Gombrowicz informed "the dumb Aniela" in his second letter to her, written in France, "and in interviews I often use your saying, Aniela, 'The story's been read, so now use your head!' which also stands at the end of *Ferdydurke*."

But the most touching part of *The Young Master of Małoszyce* comes in the letters to his family: to his brothers, Janusz and Jerzy, and after their death to his niece Teresa. Of the letters to his mother only one has survived, the rest were destroyed at his request because, "I had to hold myself back in those letters" so as not to upset her. Here is a Gombrowicz no longer posing, playing games, pretending. The dramatic quality of those letters lies in their ordinariness. They are pedestrian, like the letters of an ordinary émigré. About health and money. All of them, Janusz, Rena, Mother, were barely making ends meet. Janusz bought and sold plastic raincoats. From time to time Witold managed to send them twenty or thirty dollars with instructions on how to divide it among brothers, sister, and mother. He was having a hard time himself. "I am able to survive winters sitting by my little tile stove, a real luxury item I have treated myself to recently," he wrote in July 1959. By that time *Ferdydurke* had already come out in a French translation; two years earlier the first volume of his *Diary* had been published in Polish by the Paris-based Instytut Literacki. And sitting by that "luxurious" tile stove in far-off Argentina Gombrowicz wrote page after page of his *Diary* and of his novel *Pornografia*.

He came back to Europe to die. He realized that for the first time when, during an unfortunate stay in Berlin, the smell of the wet tree leaves reminded him of Poland so close by. And approaching death is present on all the pages of the last volume of his *Diary,* especially on the pages that became increasingly blank. And clear awareness of death—who wrote about clarity at the hour of death? Kierkegaard?—was already apparent in his letters from Vence. "In a dream I had I saw you all, the whole family together for the first time since the war, in a place that looked like Wsoła, and I was there too. Everybody was remembering what one had been through but we could not hear each other. Then suddenly Pascal himself had appeared from nowhere and said: one lives alone and dies alone."

Of his entire family only his niece Teresa visited him in Vence. But the word "visited" is perhaps not right here. Witold

and Rita waited for her at the airport in Nice. It had been thirty
years since Witold had seen anyone from his family. And during all that time only once had he talked with his brother Janusz
on the phone, but neither was able to say a word. Maybe emotion left them speechless or perhaps the connection was bad.
On the evening of Teresa's arrival they were to have dinner at a
local restaurant. But Witold had an asthma attack and the dinner reservation had to be canceled. The only talk they had was
on the way from the Nice airport to Vence. Teresa's visa was
good for only ten days. "The whole trip was only to see his illness and slow agony." Witold died almost exactly one year after her visit.

2

The only thing left behind by Gombrowicz was the pipe he
used to puff on during his asthma attacks. It is now in Teresa's
possession. Rita gave it to her. She gave his typewriter to his
Parisian nephew. It has Polish keys and is of no use to anyone.
And the children smashed the keys. Nothing has been left behind after Schulz. Nothing material that is. But the house on
Floriańska Street where Schulz lived in Drohobycz is still standing, or at least it was until recently. And you can find the corner of Czacki Street and Mickiewicz Street, where Schulz was
shot and killed during a Gestapo "action" on 19 November
1942. It was then in the very center of the ghetto, next to the
Judenrat's offices. In a photograph from the twenties we see on
that very corner a haberdasher's shop and nearby a restaurant
called Maryla. This photograph from fifty years ago and
another one showing Schulz's house are included in Jerzy
Ficowski's recent book on Schulz entitled *The Neighborhood of
the Cinnamon Shops.*

This is Ficowski's fourth book of excavations. The word
"excavation" is not used here as a metaphor; Ficowski's dogged

search for Schulz's lost letters over a period of almost four decades can be compared only to the archaeologist's patient and time-consuming sifting of the sands on the ruins of Babylon, in the Negev, and among the Mayan tombs to find fragments of vases, sometimes an earring, or only buried bones. "In the summer of 1966," Ficowski writes, "I began the search; a group of workers from the Archaeological Museum in Łódź, armed with shovels, in my presence dug up the entire courtyard referred to as the 'garden' in Maria Chazen's letters, where there is not a single tree now. Not one of Schulz's letters was found." Maria Chazen, who before the war lived in Łódź, was a pianist. For many years she and Schulz were united by "an intense, unusual friendship," as she wrote in a letter to him. (At the beginning of the war she buried all Schulz's letters to her in the courtyard of her house.) Józefina Szelińska, Schulz's fiancée, just before her flight from Janów, near Lvov, "tied all Bruno's letters in a bundle and hid them in the attic of her parent's house. Learning from Poles being repatriated from the USSR that the house had survived the war, in 1965 I was finally able to make the trip, hoping to find the letters in the attic." But the house was no more. Shortly after the war it was burned to the ground by Ukrainian bands. By far the most personal and most extensive block of Schulz's letters, over two hundred in all, had gone up in smoke.

To Debora Vogel, the now-forgotten author of a single book, *The Acacias Are Blooming,* Schulz must have written very intensively, since, as he confessed, "those letters gradually became *Cinnamon Shops" (The Street of Crocodiles* in English translation). Debora, along with her husband, mother, and four-year-old son, was gunned down in a vast "liquidation" action against the Jews of Lvov. A couple of pages from her letters to Bruno were found in 1945 in the attic of the Vogels' house by the engineer Schreier, a former pupil of Schulz. When, years later, Ficowski was finally able to reach the house, he was told that "the entire basement filled with papers left by the former tenants" was cleared out during holiday housecleaning and all the "papers" were burned.

Anna Płockier, the last of Schulz's lyric friendships and fascinations, was murdered by Ukrainian militia in Borysław. A mutual friend of the pair found Bruno's letters to Anna scattered on the floor in the Płockiers' deserted house: "How sad to think that at 30 Mazeppa Street [Anna's address in Borysław] where I have spent so many wonderful hours, no one will be left, and it will all be legend. I don't know why I feel guilty toward myself, as if I had lost something and it was my own fault." This is from the last of Bruno's letters to Anna that has been found. It is dated 19 November 1941, exactly a year to the day before the author of *The Sanatorium under the Sign of the Hourglass* was killed in nearby Drohobycz.

The location of Schulz's grave is unknown. Ficowski must conduct his wake in a nonexistent Jewish cemetery. But even if the bodies of the murdered Jews had been buried there, the cemetery itself would have disappeared. In his book *Zmut,* Rymkiewicz saved from oblivion the names of women whom the young students adored and loved: a Johasia and a Rozalka (the one who in Tuhanowicze helped Maryla, Mickiewicz's romantic love, button her dress) and that peasant girl who would tuck up her skirt while washing the floor of the room Mickiewicz had been renting and was astonished that he would not even look at her. Schulz's world—his family, friends, women, and pupils—seems to be buried much deeper in the sands. Schulz's biography consists of empty spaces, like paintings that are only frames. And even if some faded photographs have survived, they can rarely be identified.

In Ficowski's *Book of Letters* there is a photograph from August 1938 in which Schulz is seen in a garden kneeling on the grass. Next to him are two smiling young women. Behind them a friend, in a partially unbuttoned shirt, is lying on a deck

chair. Schulz is wearing a white shirt and dark tie, as in all ex-
tant photographs of him. One of the young women, in a polka-
dot dress, her knees uncovered, is Anna Płockier. The other sitting next to Bruno was known to Ficowski only by her first
name: Laura. Laura is often mentioned in Bruno's letters, and it
seems that Bruno was trying to get a publisher for her poetry or
prose. Laura and Bruno were apparently very close. After
many years her last name was unexpectedly rescued from the
ashes of oblivion in 1979, in a letter sent to Ficowski from Soviet Georgia written in a mixture of Russian and Polish. "I have
received your letter and enclosed photograph. . . . In this photograph the woman sitting next to Bruno is in fact my sister
Laura Würzberg. I immediately recognized not only my sister
but also the gold bracelet on her left hand, which was a family
heirloom." Laura Würzberg was killed during the liquidation of
the Drohobycz Jews.

Schulz started to work on *The Book of Idolatry,* a cycle of
engravings done in a technique known as *cliché-verre,* in the
early twenties, before he became a teacher in Drohobycz and
before he started to write. Several of these drawings, which
Witkiewicz called "the work of a near genius" and compared to
Goya's *Caprichos,* are in Ficowski's *Book of Letters* and *The
Neighborhood.* The complete *Book of Idolatry* has recently appeared in French, Polish, and English editions (*The Drawings of
Bruno Schulz,* Northwestern University Press, 1990). It is a
startling cycle of sexual obsessions and myths showing
dwarfish men whose faces, always resembling Schulz's own,
are frozen in a grimace of ecstasy and humiliation. The fetish of
these idolaters is a black stocking, a high-heeled slipper, and a
whip. These scenes of a mythical ritual of elemental sexuality
often have Drohobycz as a background: the town hall, the
streets, the lighted gas lamps. The menacing and towering female deities drawn by Schulz with a faultless, cool line, etched
by the fascination of humiliation which is the highest form of

desire, have the faces and bodies of the women of Drohobycz. *The Book of Idolatry* is a book of the murdered, the trace left of their existence. Often the sole trace left. As Ficowski wrote:

> In this panorama of shadows the nameless recovers his name. On many of Schulz's pictures we recognize his own face. . . . Amidst the pictures of imperious and naked women there gaze out at us the faces of the Drohobycz women admired by Schulz: Mila Lustig seated in a carriage or strolling through the enchanted town of *The Book of Idolatry;* Tynka Kupferberg keeping pace with Mila on those paths; Kuzia, a snub-nosed Ukrainian girl, her face marked with an exciting touch of vulgarity; Fryderyka Wegner, the proprietress of the most beautiful legs in all of Drohobycz and for that reason the object of special adoration, known as Undula and the main heroine of the idolatrous drawings.

In *Cinnamon Shops* a universal mythology of the Father, at times derived from the Bible, is indissolubly, almost carnally linked to a private mythology and its obsession—almost the equivalent of Kafka's vision—in which the father of a race of peacocks, pheasants, and pelicans wages an eternal battle with the cockroach clan. "At center stage we see the enigmatic figure of 'Father,' a merchant by profession, who presides over a cotton goods shop, holding sway over a swarm of darkhaired and redheaded clerks."

Like no one else, Ficowski is extraordinarily sensitive to the mythology of Schulzland; he unearths real places and real faces. Empty frames are filled with the shadows of the departed. "The store known under the sign of 'Henrietta Schulz' was located at No. 12 Drohobycz Market Square, on the corner of Mickiewicz Street, next to Józef Hammermann's jewelry store. 'I used to see Jakub Schulz,' remembers one of the now departed, 'sitting in front of the store, usually in summer and usually before noon on Sundays. The store was officially closed for business, but Jakub would be there to greet his clients who had come from Borysław.' "

When I was a child, my father owned a coal yard at Twarda or Żelazna Street just on the border of Warsaw's Jewish district. It was a wholesale business; the coal was transported in horse-drawn carts. And I remember my father coming home in the evening, his hands covered with coal dust. Nothing more. And I would give a great deal if I could meet one of those men who used to see my father sitting in front of his coal business, greeting his clients just as Jakub Schulz greeted his.

During the war years, Ficowski came into possession of three of Bruno Schulz's letters to Andrzej Pleśniewicz. I knew Pleśniewicz before the war. He had a dark birthmark on his right cheek; it ran in the family. Pleśniewicz was killed in February 1945 on his way back to Warsaw after the wanderings that followed the uprising of 1944. Pleśniewicz belonged to Gombrowicz's table at the Zodiak café in Warsaw. Of all the people from that table at the Zodiak (I too was one of them at a later point), only Ewa, the widow of one of my old friends, is among the living.

These two books of memory, as insubstantial as writing on water, I read as my own prehistory from a world that was but is no more.

Translated by Jadwiga Kosicka

KANTOR'S KADDISH

I attended the first rehearsal at the Akademie der Künste. It was four or five days after Tadeusz Kantor's arrival in Berlin with his latest play. The rows of seats were steeply banked, as in an amphitheater. The house was full, the way it would be at a premiere. People of all ages. For a moment I had the feeling that I knew them all. That I had seen them all somewhere before. And that these were the same people who always come to see Kantor at La Mama or in Milan.

On stage, there was Kantor wearing the same black suit as always. But I don't remember whether in previous productions he had a white scarf. And it seemed to me his soft felt hat was new. For me Kantor has always been a Charon, but now he celebrated the ritual of prodding the dead in a gentler manner than usual, with a kind of heartbreaking sadness, as though he were in a great hurry for all of them to go away once and for all. As though he were saying farewell to himself.

There were four doors at the back of the stage. And through those four doors, which were constantly being opened and shut, the characters of the play would race frantically about in a circle, panting, sometimes only stopping for a moment, as if they were chasing one another or trying to escape: the priest from *Wielopole, Wielopole* with a cross in his hand and the skirts of his cassock sweeping the stage; the waiter carrying a carafe on a tray; the Hasidic twin brothers; the cleaning woman with enormous breasts that kept spilling out of her apron—taken directly from Goya—who would wipe the floor with a rag and constantly run back and forth from washing the floor to the waiter and the priest and then run over to Kantor as if she were asking him about something. Then through the middle door there would appear and disappear a military band in shakos and braided uniforms from before World War I. They all played violins and goose-stepped in a parade march. A little Jew from a Chagall painting sprang out of nowhere and started to conduct. The band disappeared through the door again, but the little Jew in the yarmulke kept conducting for a while in silence. Now Kantor was yelling at the sound technician hidden somewhere close to the ceiling beyond the highest row of seats.

I did not stay to the end of the rehearsal, but I felt I had grasped the principle of movement. The characters would appear and disappear like figures on Renaissance and baroque church or town-hall clocks, where Death with a scythe often keeps company with saints and kings. Or as on ornate music boxes where the tiny figurines jerk and revolve to the same merry tune repeated over and over again. The doors open and close, the characters appear and disappear, but by the time the performance was half over, I already knew that the doors would finally close on all the characters and on Kantor's theater, never to open again. And right then I suddenly understood: *I Shall Never Return.*

Before the performance, the tables and chairs on stage are stacked one on top of another, as in a restaurant at daybreak, before the first customers have appeared. The waiter, with a towel over his arm, arranges the chairs and methodically measures the distance between the tables with a tape measure. He gently nudges the priest, who has fallen asleep with his head slumped on an empty table. Or perhaps it is the waiting room of a railway station? But where? At what station?

By now a podium has been fashioned out of two tables, one placed on the top of the other, and a gentleman wearing an evening jacket, his bow tie askew, has climbed up and launches into a speech to the people, glancing from time to time at a crumpled sheet of paper full of holes. What kind of a speech is it? He stammers and only a few disconnected words can be heard. The next moment all the doors fly open and in bursts a ragtag band of men and women with bundles, suitcases, baskets. Among them is the priest from *Wielopole, Wielopole* with the white cross, and the twin Hasidic brothers with a rectangular parcel like a rolled-up rug which they won't let go of for a moment. I thought it was a rolled-up Torah, but Kantor calls it "the plank of last resort." In this swarm of bodies, rags, and packages, in a monochromatic palette of browns, grays, and blacks, in this horrifying, quivering ballet in a railway waiting room at the hour of flight one can recognize—deeply imprinted in one's memory and as if salvaged from a theatrical museum— not only characters and figures from Kantor's previous productions but props as well: an old-fashioned camera that turns into a machine gun from World War I, a trough in which a man-rat with an enormous bandaged phallus is lying, and a chicken coop from which there emerges a young woman in black panties and bra who cackles like a hen, perhaps the Princess Kremlinska from Witkacy's *Dainty Shapes and Hairy Apes,* or *The Water Hen* interpreted at last as a materialized metaphor. There is also rolled out a gallows on wheels, and a mannequin/double of the waiter with a towel over his arm standing motionless on a small platform in the center door. And in this dreamlike mixture of bodies, costumes, and props Kantor stands, lost in thought, sometimes as though he were somewhere else, but this theater of ever-returning apparitions that he has called forth has this time gripped him, as if he had ceased to control it, as if it had totally engulfed him. For the first time Kantor leaves the stage—swirling with its merry-go-round of bodies—and returns, through a door that will open and shut for him, with a black coffin. He will caress it like a violin and carry it with him almost to the very end.

The cleaning woman with the breasts spilling out now brings Kantor a tattered overcoat and a battered wide-brimmed hat. Or perhaps it is not the cleaning woman but one of the characters in *Wielopole, Wielopole* whom Kantor calls the Exiled Convict from Siberia. Now this exile's coat will be put on the waiter. Next Kantor pulls the hat down over the waiter's forehead and wraps a shawl around his neck. The waiter is now called Odysseus, and some lines from Wyspiański's *Return of Odysseus* are heard as if coming from afar. But even Polish eyes and ears cannot always distinguish the ghosts and apparitions of the Polish theater from Kantor's own ghosts and apparitions. The transformed waiter resembles a scarecrow. And this scarecrow will be one of the figures of death until the end of the performance.

In Kantor's theater the sign/theatrical image often has a complex and not always clear symbolic function. But as in Fellini it gets under one's eyelids, comes back in dreams, and is in and of itself an icon, like the figure of Christ suspended on wires from the airplane circling over Rome or the sea monster on the beach at dawn in *8½*. All of a sudden the stage becomes empty. A moment later the Hasidic twins run in, wearing the purple cassocks and miters worn by cardinals and dancing an Argentine tango. They disappear but the tango is now danced by the priest from *Wielopole, Wielopole* holding the cross as if it were his partner. Time and time again the Hasidic cardinals and the priest would appear still dancing the same tango from a dream.

I was very tired during the Berlin rehearsal and may have dozed off once or twice. But my dozing off was not in vain. In that dream I dreamed there swarmed a multitude of characters, mannequins, and stage props: the gynecological table with broken legs, the cradle, and the dry crackling of the rattle announcing the feast of Purim from *Wielopole, Wielopole*. And perhaps it was during that short nap that I grasped yet another truth in *I Shall Never Return*. I am afraid to follow this truth to its logical conclusion. There are such moments—sometimes not even so very frightful—when one's whole life comes back in the single beat of a dream. These are moments of dim (or are they bright?) awareness preceding the end.

Shortly before the end of the performance on the piled-up tables and chairs the actors and their mannequins sit very close together as if glued to one another, the way they did on the school benches in *The Dead Class*. The priest calls out the names and surnames of the dead. For the last time Kantor celebrates his ritual of Forefathers' Eve. Marian Kantor's name is also called out in this roll call of the dead.

Once again the stage becomes empty. And once again the two Hasidic Jews burst in with their Torah of "last resort" tightly wrapped in paper, and the priest from *Wielopole, Wielopole* with his ubiquitous cross, the women carrying enormous bundles, the big-city ladies in tattered furs, the salesmen with bulging suitcases tied with string. Someone screams something, someone points to the sky to indicate that something is drawing near. But what? Or who? And from what direction? Some dates are mentioned: the year 1945. This despairing flight, repeated over and over, stubbornly and obsessively invokes all the flights heading nowhere and all the deportations, from the Urals to the Oder River.

The performance is almost over. Someone is shooting at the crowd, using the old-fashioned camera transformed into a machine gun. Making a wide sweep. Methodically and systematically. Until no one remains alive. The bodies fall one on top of the other and "a still life of the dead" is formed out of corpses, suitcases, bundles, and "the plank of last resort." Now enter the elegant mourners/gravediggers in top hats and cutaways. Slowly and precisely they spread black shrouds over the huge mound of corpses, keeping time with the rising and falling beat of the Rakoczy March from Berlioz's oratorio *The Damnation of Faust.* The priest's white cross remains visible for a while, sticking out above the mass grave, only to disappear a moment later into the sea of black shrouds. The funeral shrouds are in all the hues of black, as in those large canvases of Goya housed in the Prado Museum in Madrid which are seldom reproduced. The only thing I could find comparable to Kantor's vision of the world would be the cruelty of Goya's *Caprichos.* But that was not the end. The cleaning woman, who, on her knees with her skirts tucked up, had followed the military band, humming the old Hasidic chant "Ani aamin," now crawls under the shrouds and slowly begins pulling out the corpses buried underneath. To the very last one. She drags them offstage and the doors now close after them for the very last time. She won't wash the floor anymore. She slowly climbs the deserted podium. She opens her mouth. She wants to say something. But not a word comes out.

At the end of the last performance, when the prolonged applause had finally died out, the indomitable La Mama herself, Ellen Stewart, came on stage: "Next summer Kantor will return with his *Dead Class.*"

Translated by Jadwiga Kosicka

KANTOR, MEMORY, MEMOIRE (1915–90)

T he setting is a bombed-out railway station on the river Oder, three or four weeks after the end of World War II. Our narrator is Bohdan Korzeniewski, one of the most important theater people in postwar Poland, who during the German occupation worked as a librarian at the Warsaw University Library.[1] His dogged pursuit of the rare books and priceless theatrical collections stolen by the Germans from the Polish National Library has brought him to this Silesian railway station, now a part of Poland. Korzeniewski has already located the books in the Reich, where they survived the war intact in the basements of castles belonging to the German aristocracy, and he has packed them in crates and sent them to Poland via Russian military transports. At that time the "newly recovered Polish territories" were still under Soviet occupation.

The transport with the books and other spoils of war had stopped for the night in this small Silesian town and was to resume its journey the next morning, but Korzeniewski, the future theoretician and theater practitioner, was so worried about the cargo in his charge that he was unable to sleep. When he arrived at the station to check whether everything was in order, he was puzzled by the strange noises issuing from the cars of the long train: ticking, clicking, buzzing, occasionally punctuated by the sound of chimes or the cuckoo. The cars, as it turned out, were loaded with all kinds of clocks. Some still ticking and striking the hours. Suddenly a drunken Russian officer appeared from nowhere, reached for his gun, and started to shoot at the cars with the chiming clocks.

Had that drunken officer done the shooting at those bourgeois cuckoo clocks, not with his gun, but with an antique camera with a long protruding pipe, we would have unexpectedly found ourselves in Kantor's theater. In that actual setting on the platform of a small railway station somewhere in Silesia remembered half a century later by an eyewitness, we recognize the familiar non-cohesion and non-continuity of objects and events that we usually think of as the exclusive discovery of surrealist and postsurrealist painting and poetry.

That long train loaded with clocks still ticking and chiming the hours may appear as a captivating set for an as yet unwritten play for the theater of the absurd, but this vision of the absurd, to be discovered by the theater in the 1950s, was already being played out on that small Silesian railway platform. *La réalité dépasse la fiction*. On top of the crates with the priceless rare books pilfered by the Germans from occupied Warsaw, the clocks looted from a small German town chime romantic carillons in a Russian military transport heading east. The props become signs. In Kantor's theater the props become signs of memory. It is "memorized" history.

This time the setting is a baroque cathedral in Poznań, also in the first few weeks after the liberation. The narrator is once again Bohdan Korzeniewski, the future director of *The Undivine Comedy* and *Don Juan*. The cathedral's vault had been shattered by a bomb, and snowflakes from a late May squall were whirling through a gaping hole in the middle nave.

The blast must have been powerful, Korzeniewski tells us, since the baroque statues fell off the altars. They were strewn about the tiled floor in such strange positions. Here and there, as in medieval paintings of decapitated martyrs, a statue clutched in its hands its own head, which had fallen off. But it turned out those weren't statues but cadavers dragged out of the cathedral tombs. Some were quite well preserved, often with skin still attached to the skulls, robbed of jewelry but with scraps of rich silks and cloth of gold stuck here and there. A hideous orgy must have taken place, because the women's cadavers had their leg bones spread apart and male skeletons placed on top of them.

In that baroque cathedral the desecrated cadavers seen by the flickering light streaming through colored panes of shattered stained-glass windows seemed to have been called forth to enact a medieval Dance of Death. In that cathedral destroyed by artillery shells the statues of the martyred saints become the doubles of the martyred dead. In Kantor's theater the dead are the doubles of the living and the living are the doubles of the dead.

For hundreds of years the inhabitants of the tiny Mexican town of Guanajouata buried their dead in a muddy mountain slope. Desperately poor, they could not afford coffins. Not many years ago during one of the frequent earthquakes, which along with poverty are a permanent feature of that province, the mummified cadavers fell out of the side of the mountain. *Las momias pequeñas del mundo* (as they are called by the natives) are now on display in a local museum, "buried" in glass cases. In this Mexican Pompeii of the destitute, one can view the little bodies of children, their mouths still wide open as if caught by surprise, the corpses of women still wearing black stockings on legs covered with skin, the bodies of men with protruding

phalluses frozen forever in erection. But perhaps the most horrifying are the female and male heads that had become detached
during the quake, still wearing headbands or kerchiefs, their
teeth bared in an eternal grimace. Death here is as obscene as it
was in the baroque cathedral in Poznań with its desecrated
vaults. In this Dance of Death the dead are always grinning. To
this very day, during carnival processions and festivities in Sicily, in the squares of Madrid and Barcelona, in distant Rio de
Janeiro and the remotest poverty-stricken towns and villages of
Mexico, the death masks march alongside the nuptial masks,
just as they did centuries ago during the Roman Saturnalia.

In Kantor's theater the dead return to take once again their
seats on the school benches. They push aside the doubles of
their childhood and drag them offstage. The class has been dead
for years, the doubles are mannekins. In *Wielopole, Wielopole* the
recruits in World War I uniforms, who have been goose-
stepping to the beat of a parade march, a minute later become
sallow-faced mannekins thrown into a mass grave. The double
of the bridesmaid, still in her white wedding gown and veil, lies
motionless, her legs now spread apart after having been raped
repeatedly by a group of soldiers. The prelate and uncle in
Wielopole, Wielopole, from Kantor's family saga, who has joined
the young couple in marriage and blessed the recruits going off
to the war, will be hanged on the massive cross rolled onstage
in a blasphemous evocation of Christ's passion. In Kantor's theater death is violated and the *sacrum* desecrated. *Cette tragique
farce* is the term used by Rabelais in book 4, chapter 13 of *Gar-
gantua and Pantagruel.* Rabelais seems to have been the inventor
of the term, applied to the profanation of an Easter mystery
play put on by François Villon. Villon told the boys disguised
as devils to frighten a Franciscan friar who had refused to lend
his cape and stole to the old peasant playing God the father. The
band of noisy young devils waylaid the friar riding on the con-
vent filly and scared them both out of their wits.

In Kantor's tragifarce, just as in Beckett's tragifarces (despite all the differences in their semantics and their imagery, one cannot help seeing profound similarities between these two theaters representative of the century's end), birth is *already* dying. In *The Dead Class* birthing takes place on a broken dentist's chair, and in *Endgame* dying takes place in a garbage can. In both their theaters birth and death are degraded.

Because Kantor was always present onstage from beginning to end and often goaded his actors with an impatient snap of the fingers, I have compared him to Charon, who ferries the dead across the river Styx to the land of forgetfulness. But Kantor was a Charon who ferried the dead back again to our side across the river of memory. It little matters that he brought them back for scarcely an hour and as their own doubles/mannekins. In the Polish folk tradition a cemetery is called "a park for stiffs."

Kantor/Charon in his black suit and soft felt hat is memory incarnate: memory of childhood and memory of family. Memory of a room that once *was*, re-created onstage out of a few wooden planks ("only we are missing from that room"), and even memory of the sound of the rattle in the real Wielopole, shaken by the village boys on Good Friday. In Kantor's theater of obsessive memory everything reappears: school benches, faded family photographs, and the name and surname of his father, Marian Kantor, read aloud in a roll call of the dead in *I Shall Never Return*.

One would have to be deaf not to hear in Kantor's work the theme of biography as a graveyard. Kantor's theater renders visible the shadow cast by a world that has been forever effaced and can return only at odd times when doggedly summoned by the importuning of memory—hence those swelling bursts of deafening music that ebb away into silence, like the Viennese waltz in *The Dead Class,* or, in different registers, the Jewish lullabies and old Hasidic chants invoked by painful yet tender remembrance.

In the theater of memory of Charon the ferryman there always reappear familiar motifs and personages from all of Kantor's productions, starting with the earliest at his theater Cricot II in Cracow: the male and female mannekins with exposed genitals and a bawdy hen in a chicken coop. Duchamp's famous urinal has become an objet d'art for all time, but in Kantor's theater the broken dentist's chair that serves as a birthing stool and the pail into which the cleaning woman wrings dirty water out of her rag never become objets d'art. They may have been intended to provoke a reaction in audiences, but not of the sort favored by aesthetes. And this is what makes Kantor different.

The ordinary, mortal human comedy is played out amid this surprising jumble of coops for human fowl, broken cradles, portable gallows on wheels, and rugs rolled up like the holy Torah, just as it once happened at that railway station at the end of the war in the unexpected proximity of those stolen cuckoo clocks and the looted rare books from Warsaw libraries. In this quintessential Polish theater in which echo-images, echo-symbols, and echo-quotations from Mickiewicz and Witkiewicz, Wyspiański and Gombrowicz, are juxtaposed and create a strange amalgam, Kantor's new mortal human comedy is absolutely universal.

Kantor's theater is a wandering troupe, perhaps the only one left in our time. Making it—quite surprisingly—similar to the Elizabethan players who wandered for months on end along the Baltic through the cities of the Hanseatic League (and who even during Shakespeare's lifetime went from Königsberg to Cracow with three of his plays), transporting in huge horse-drawn wagons their rich costumes, armor, and even a cage with the head of a decapitated rebel. Kantor's theater is also akin in its wanderings to Molière's first company, which, journeying from palaces to country inns, likewise transported by wagon their *commedia* costumes and freshly written manuscripts of plays, alongside the powders and paints for whitening and rouging the performers' faces. They had a cradle too, since Molière's first company, just like Kantor's troupe now, was an extended family. In my mind's eye I can easily picture Kantor's theater in horse-drawn wagons on its way from Cracow to Paris.

I have seen Kantor's productions in Nancy, Florence, and Berlin as well as at La Mama in New York. I have even met ardent fans of his theater who went wandering along after Kantor like geese behind a cart or seagulls in the wake of a ship. Obviously such a theater must offer real nourishment that, even if bitter, is unlike anything else to be seen in the whole wide world. Perhaps this is the case because Kantor, like very few artists in our time, succeeded in translating into theatrical signs a forgotten memory that is locked away in each and every one of us like a healed wound. And perhaps this was precisely the cathartic role played by Kantor/Charon who brings back the dead.

The last Polish Charon of contemporary world theater, Kantor already is and will remain only a memory. But this memory contains more than death: there is birth. And birth is the negation of death. Memory is always life-giving. A return of the dead to the living.

Note

¹ The following account is taken from Małgorzata Szejnert, *Sława i infamia: Rozmowy z Bohdanem Korzeniewskim* (Glory and infamy: conversations with Bohdan Korzeniewski) (London: Aneks, 1988).

Translated by Jadwiga Kosicka

MROŻEK'S *EMIGRÉS*

During my stay in Berlin I lived right next to the Kottbusser Damm subway station. It was a branch of the main line that went to the center of town and to Kudam. But from where I lived Kudam seemed very far away, almost in another city. Just around the corner from my street there was a canal gently winding among the osier bushes and bordered by small rocky beaches. Every day I saw people lying there, sunning themselves in the warm May sun.

From the very first I liked my neighborhood. At the turn of the century it had been a bohemian quarter. In the sixties the hippies took it over. Now it was the quarter inhabited by the Turks and the punks. Tightly wrapped in kerchiefs and stiffly erect as though they were carrying jars of water on their heads, the women strolled through the quarter with two or three small children by their side. Young girls in long bright-colored skirts played hopscotch or jumped rope in the middle of the street, paying no attention to the passing cars. They all had the same deep, dark eyes, slightly filmed over with a prematurely grown-up look. Men in caps sat on benches pulled out in the street in front of the *bierstubes*. They drank beer and drew on hand-rolled cigarettes.

Most of the signposts, posters, and advertisements were in both German and Turkish. But the walls were covered with strange colored swirls and some kind of hieroglyphs put everywhere by other inhabitants of the neighborhood. Among the Turkish women gliding along like huge caterpillars and their black mustachioed men there would unexpectedly appear a band of scantily dressed young boys and girls, with one earring or a pearl stuck in the nose, heads cleanly shaved except for a comblike tuft of green or purple hair standing up in the middle. If you followed the gentle windings of the canal, where small barges loaded with timber slowly floated with the current, you could reach the Berlin Wall in less than half an hour. I had seen the Wall for the first time ten years before. It had been pointed out to me in utter horror. And it did look forbidding in its depressing grayness. But this time I could barely recognize it. The entire length and breadth of the wall was covered with graffiti in gaudy oranges, greens, and blues, like New York City subway cars. Punk civilization had taken possession of the wall in West Berlin.

When Mieczysław Czechowicz and Andrzej Łapicki came from Warsaw to Berlin with Mrożek's *Emigrés* for a single night, the auditorium with a foreign-sounding name used for the performance was in my quarter, but three or four subway stops further to the east of the center, almost in the suburbs. On the way there I got lost several times. The street was deserted, the windows of the apartment houses and warehouses dark. Finally I heard strange sounds drifting toward me from somewhere, and I saw a group of jean-clad teenagers gyrating rhythmically to a mixture of jazz and Near Eastern music in front of a building. It was a recently opened Turkish discotheque. But I had come to the right place. On the front door was a piece of cardboard with a handwritten notice in big letters proclaiming: *Emigrés*. You had to walk up two or three flights. It must have been a community center or a club transformed into a theater for that particular occasion. An improvised curtain of white bed sheets or tablecloths sown together separated the stage, or rather platform, from an auditorium of some two hundred seats. All the places were already taken, but additional chairs were constantly being added for those still arriving. I did not know anybody in the audience. But it seemed to me that they all knew one another. The men clapped each other on the back, some even ceremoniously kissed women's hands. Several families had brought their children, having no one to leave them with. The men as well as the women were festively dressed in bright colors, but it looked as though the clothes had just been bought. They must all have been recent émigrés.

I had seen Mrożek's *Emigrés* on the stage only once before. It was some ten years ago, and I don't recall whether I saw it at Stony Brook or at some small college in Connecticut not far from New Haven. It was directed by a bright young man who had come to America two years earlier, married an American girl, and now taught theater there. He also played the role of the intellectual, AA.

The earlier production was not half-bad, but the audience, consisting of students and a few professors, seemed at a loss to understand what the play was about. I didn't understand everything either. The issue of *Dialog* containing the play had gone astray and I did not know the play. I watched rather than listened, since the actors' diction left something to be desired. The role of ZZ, the acquisitive newcomer in the land of plenty, was played by a chubby young actor in striped overalls. The political refugee wore wide baggy pants held up by suspenders and a black unbuttoned vest. Despite his young years, he was already balding, and for some unknown reason his face was plastered with a thick layer of powder. And then suddenly I realized that these were two clowns: the redheaded and the white-faced, the strong and the weak, the boor and the snob in yet another version of the nineteenth-century circus tradition that has been repeated endlessly ever since. It seemed to me that Mrożek was even taking his gags from the circus. But when the redhead took his shoes off and exposed the holes in his socks, I recognized yet another source and yet another model. Mrożek's two clowns were Vladimir and Estragon. They try to go their separate ways, but can't. They try to leave, but can't. Where could they go? They're waiting. For their Godot. The Godot I know only too well. I waited for him too.

In that Berlin performance, when after several attempts the curtain made out of the soiled tablecloths or bed sheets finally went up, it disclosed a shallow platform turned into a stage on which stood chairs of the kind that had been brought into the auditorium a few minutes ago for extra seats and a table of the kind that had been brought into the snack bar a few minutes ago for serving beer. Łapicki and Czechowicz sat on the chairs. Łapicki's face was powdered white, Czechowicz's face was tanned, and maybe I was imagining it but I would have sworn he had big red freckles. But they were not circus clowns and no one laughed when Czechowicz opened the can of dog food. Or even when he showed the holes in his socks. But someone sitting behind me said in a loud whisper to the person next to him: "We haven't sunk that low yet."

No one laughed even once during the entire performance. As if they were watching the émigrés on stage unwillingly. But that's not quite the right word. Rather, embarrassedly. As if they had suddenly realized they could have played the part themselves. But not both the roles. Only that of ZZ, who spends his spare time at the train station because it's free and besides, where else could he go? On the same street, near the theater, there was a railway station and the entire performance was punctuated with the rattling of passing trains.

After the performance I pulled open the homemade tablecloth curtains and went up on the "stage." Czechowicz and Łapicki were still sitting in their chairs. They were stunned to see me. I too was deeply moved. And for a moment the three of us might have imagined that time had been set back twenty years and that I, as a Warsaw theater critic, had gone backstage to congratulate two brilliant Warsaw actors for a brilliant performance. But there was little time for emotion. Czechowicz and Łapicki had to catch the train. They brought us tea in beer mugs from the snack bar. But that wasn't the only thing that tasted bitter. As we drank our tea the three of us suddenly realized not only that the audience for this Berlin performance of *Emigrés* was composed of "guest workers" but that the Polish theater itself had become a "guest worker."

It still wasn't late and I was in no hurry to get home. I walked back along the canal. I came to the Wall. It was a moonless night. The Wall was black and gloomy again.

August 1988

Translated by Jadwiga Kosicka

GROTOWSKI, OR
THE LIMIT

A postcard I received a couple of months ago from Alexander Verlag, my German publisher, shows Jerzy Grotowski sitting side by side with Peter Brook. There is a blank wall behind them. They are sitting on chairs that have been placed together, or perhaps they are wooden benches. As in the waiting room of a railway station. But where? At what station? A large, bulging knapsack is lying at their feet. To which of the two does it belong? Brook is wearing a black suit and a turtleneck sweater. His head is slightly bent over, his immense forehead sloping back into the almost bald dome of his skull, with tufts of hair only along the sides. Grotowski is also wearing a black suit, but he has on an unbuttoned shirt and trousers with suspenders. His bare feet are thrust into sandals. For a moment one might think that Vladimir and Estragon have met again and are waiting for a new Godot.

Both Grotowski and Brook have traveled a lot. It might be better to say: they have wandered. Brook's travels, like everything else he has done, are well documented: descriptions,

reports, photographs. Of Grotowski's wanderings—who for
months would trek alone through the vast expanses of India—
the only trace left is what he carries within him. Brook, in his
travels to the ends of the earth, always insatiable for theatrical-
ity, was relentlessly searching in inaccessible villages of Africa
and Asia for new ways to enrich the theater: an undiscovered
gesture or musical instrument or melody. Who can ever forget
the ribbons, taken from the Kabuki, which entwine the lovers
in *A Midsummer Night's Dream;* the arrows in the *Mahabharata,*
suspended in midair, which may never have been released from
the bent bow; or the bonfires that the old woman lights in the
three corners of the world for Carmen and her last lover around
their love bed? In Brook's productions fire, water, and sand are
thrilling signs; these symbols never lose materiality. The red
sand in the *Mahabharata* was actually brought from the banks of
the Ganges. Like no other artist, Brook has turned ritual into
theater. Whereas Grotowski stubbornly and persistently tried to
turn theater back into ritual. Until he finally realized that for
true believers such an attempt is sacrilege, pillage of the *sacrum,*
and for nonbelievers a form of cheating, and that in Cieslak's
self-flagellation in *The Constant Prince* martyrdom is mere
acting.

In the postcard from Germany Brook has his hands on his
knees and listens, eyes half-closed. I remember quite well how
Brook listens. He is on the alert then, like a cat. Like a hungry
cat. He says nothing, only from time to time he twists and folds
the paper napkin in his hands. That crumpled napkin turns out
to be a stage design. In the photograph Grotowski has his right
hand raised, he's looking at Brook and talking. Brook always
asks questions. Giorgio Strehler, with whom I worked on *The
Tempest,* also asks questions, but he answers them himself and
at great length. Then he asks another question, but he's interested only in his own answers. Conversation with Brook is difficult: the other person does all the talking. Conversation with

Strehler is impossible: he does all the talking. Of the three, only Grotowski is a true conversationalist. Perhaps that is why the one final thing he wants to save from traditional theater is the act of meeting. Reciprocally.

After many years I met Grotowski again in Santa Monica. He had changed considerably in comparison with the likeness on that German postcard. Over the years I have seen Grotowski alternatingly fat or thin as though his inner transformations were reflected in the bodily manifestation of his soul. In the photo Grotowski still had thick, dark hair falling in disarray over his ears and neck. Now his high forehead was prominent, his silvering hair blended with his already gray sideburns and sparse, scraggly goatee. He was wearing his usual dark suit, which was too big for him since he had lost so much weight, a white shirt, and an uncustomary old-fashioned dark tie with a thick knot. "He looks exactly like a civil servant from Galicia in the old Austro-Hungarian Empire," said L.

Grotowski gave a talk about Haitian voodoo cult. About performing the ceremony, which is a trance that infects the participants. And about how the actor is able to control the trance. In the documentary film he showed, a white rooster's head was cut off, and his feathers floated in the air.

That was almost two years ago at the Getty Center in Santa Monica, where I had been invited for a year's residency along with nine art historians and ethnographers from America and Europe. I was the only theater historian and perhaps that is why I was asked to arrange the talk for Grotowski. At that point he still spoke English with a very thick accent and the film he showed (perhaps owing to a faulty projector) kept breaking and flapping. Like the feathers of that white rooster. For years I have considered Grotowski a guru, having observed the trance he induces in his listeners, more by his personality, I think, than by anything he says. But that was always an audience of theater professionals. They came specifically "to sit at the feet of the great Grotowski." In contrast, my learned colleagues from the Getty Center had heard little or nothing of Grotowski. And when they displayed enthusiasm, it was for a sketch by Leonardo, unexpectedly discovered on the back of a well-known painting. Yet Grotowski was received enthusiastically by these art historians and ethnographers. As no one else either before him or after him that year. And there were excellent speakers among the lecturers in the series.

That evening Grotowski came to our place for Russian pierogis with cheese and potato filling. He ate with real gusto. I voiced my amazement: "You should be eating only lotus seeds." "Lotus seeds go wonderfully well with Polish vodka," he replied. For me that was a totally new Grotowski. I had never heard him make fun of himself before. He seemed to have opened up. He was lonely. For a long time now his friends and his actors have been scattered throughout the world. Or they are no longer living. Just like mine. As he was leaving, he gave me a book that he said he never parted with. It was a French translation of Martin Buber's *Tales of the Hasidim*. These tales are similar to the ones that Stanisław Vincenz collected among the Hasidic Jews who lived on the upper Czeremosz River. "Good Lord," said one of those distant and later successors of the Baal Shem Tov, "save the Jews. If you can't save them all, at least save the ones who are your own personal chosen." It was strange, but that evening I had the impression that the former guru Grotowski, absorbed in eating Russian pierogis, was one of the Hasidim.

In May or June of the same year we were invited by Grotowski to his campus at Irvine. It is one of those California university campuses located in a thick forest where buildings and men pale to insignificance. The forest changes almost imperceptibly into open land. On the other side, the ocean is only a couple of miles away. On the edge of the campus, next to an old barn he had been given, Grotowski set up a circular Siberian yurt built of bright wood. In that dark barn, in that bright yurt, in the nearby scrub, or along the seashore, for an entire year, day after day, sometimes well into the night, Grotowski kept training a new group of actors. There were seven young men and a girl. One young man was Mexican, one (I think) Malay, the rest were from various countries of the two Americas. The girl was Japanese. They came to Grotowski either on their own or at his initiative.

For that long night in Irvine, besides L. and me, Grotowski had also invited André Gregory and his wife and two or three people from the campus. So the performers outnumbered the spectators. The yurt still smelled of fresh resin, the waxed floor was as shiny as in the Japanese No theater. We took off our shoes and were seated on a wooden bench. The performance started with the young Mexican, who—Grotowski said—had absolute pitch. He began a song in which the same sequence of notes was repeated, then faded out and came back again. This singsong was accompanied by an equally monotonous dance step. The performer's knees rubbed against each other, and his toes were pointed in. At each step, given the position of his body, the performer's head and shoulders would bend down and then straighten up. This lasted a long time and gradually tension mounted. As though that strange step had stuck in each of our throats. Then the first dancer was joined by the others, all intoning the same monotonous singsong and executing the same rocking step. They resembled an uncoiling snake. There must have been something hypnotic in this snake, since the invited guests gradually joined in, repeating the nodding dance step and the chanting.

Later I asked Grotowski about the origin of this strange step so mortifying to the body. He said that it was a combination of the ritual rocking of the Hasidim and of the last of the meditative positions in Zen. Meditation requires tension of the body. And of the thinking process, which precedes action.

Then we were led out of the yurt several hundred feet into the scrub. On a small knoll facing us, two of the young men and the girl were repeating the same bowing step once again, but standing in place. They would turn in succession to the four corners of the world, and then bow to the sky and the earth. To an outside observer it might have seemed that this dance was yet another secret ritual among the hundreds of strange cults that flourish in California, but it was only two young men from Latin America and a Japanese girl standing on a small knoll while the sun was setting.

At one point three horses—two white and one black— passed in front of us. As though they had just stepped out of a Gauguin painting. Their front legs were fettered. The horses moved slowly, taking short steps, their heads bent down low in search of tufts of grass hard to find in the dry scrub. For an instant they blocked our view of the two young men and the girl, whose heads were bent low like the horses'. Later I asked Grotowski whether he had planned that moment of beauty. "No," he replied, "God is the only great director."

Then still later, at dusk, the seven young men and the girl started to run in a huge circle in front of the yurt. They ran, now faster, now slower, changing step. They did not look at one another, but they all changed step simultaneously as though they were tied by an invisible thread. It lasted a very long time, but the longer this monotonous running, this abstract and empty ballet without music, lasted the more enchanting it became. Until it finally stopped. I asked Grotowski how he measured the length of the running time. "The running stopped," he said, "when it played itself out."

Late at night we were taken back to the barn. Again we were seated on the wooden bench along one of the walls. Grotowski was squatting in the right corner. The barn was dark, except for a dozen candles that flickered on a low table directly in front of us. The performers were now running close to the walls. They kept changing, but there were always only two: the pursuer and the pursued, a man and a woman or two men. They were naked, in white shrouds hanging loosely from their bodies, with skeleton bones drawn in thick, bold lines. In the light of the candles, whose flames swayed as though mown down by the wind from the onrushing bodies, enormous shadows moved along the walls of the barn.

The pursuit was a sequence that was repeated over and over again. And it always ended in a gesture signifying rape, murder, or forgiveness. Twice, when the pursuer finally overtook his human prey, he covered it with a shroud, and twice after that the creature who had been hunted down or raped slowly lifted its head, still covered by the shroud, and froze in a half-seated position like Lazarus just risen from the dead, or, according to Grotowski's syncretism of myths and cultures, like an Egyptian mummy wrapped in white bandages slowly rising up out of a sarcophagus.

Early the next morning, as we were saying good-bye, I asked Grotowski whether he had any documentation about his work for the year—photographs, drawings, written accounts. "What for?" He seemed to be genuinely surprised. "The only lasting imprint is made on memory." Then he smiled. "You should know that best of all, Jan. You wrote about the body's memory."

That was the final year of Grotowski's work at Irvine. His new Centro di Lavoro is located in Pontedera, a small Tuscan village thirty or forty miles from Florence. There's not even a third-class restaurant in the village, so Grotowski's pupils—and there are about twenty of them—prepare their own meals. They will stay with Grotowski for three years. Shortly after the opening of this new school in the wilderness, Brook visited Grotowski. If they again sat side by side on a wooden bench, the wanderer's knapsack this time would have belonged to Brook. On this occasion Brook talked about Gordon Craig. He called Craig one of the greatest universal masters, since Craig's influence and legend have held sway throughout the entire century and embraced all aspects of theater. Craig's legend has been spread by those who knew firsthand at least one of his very few productions and passed it on to their pupils, and so from one generation to the next of pupils of pupils. The Craig legend, which has lived on after him, comprises a vision of total theater. This total theater is—and Brook didn't stress this in his lecture—an impossible theater, since its essence is neither the word nor the actor nor the setting nor the music. Perhaps it is only movement and light. I am not sure whether it was Brook who first compared Grotowski to Craig. But I think it is a revealing comparison. It says something about both of them.

Georges Banu was also present at that meeting in Pontedera. In a letter he wrote me, he said, "I saw Grotowski. What limitations he imposes! But what strength in those limitations. For the first time I experienced the limit of theater."

I experienced that limit myself two years earlier in Irvine. At sunrise, in the scrub that almost creeps up to the threshold of Grotowski's yurt—the rattlesnakes hissed and the air quivered. Such quivering air I have seen once before in the Negev by the rose columns of Solomon.

Translated by Jadwiga Kosicka

PART II

A SHORT TREATISE ON EROTICISM

Love looks not with the eyes, but with the mind.

—*A Midsummer Night's Dream*

D uring an evening with the Ionescos, Chiaromonte vented his dissatisfaction with the French *nouvelle vague*, particularly in its erotic aspect, as expressed in films and novels. He called it eroticism without a partner; as there is no partner—he said—it is really the eroticism of masturbation.

To my way of thinking, it would, perhaps, be more accurate to say that the partner does not exist as a person, as a subject. He or she has the existence and concreteness of an object. He is a thing, or rather transformed into a thing.

It is possible, however, that Chiaromonte's arguments are more philosophically complex. The partner, indeed, does not exist. He or she is being created, is nothing but an erotic vision come to life. As in masturbation he or she is being created by one's own sexual ego. But erotic imagination never creates a fully developed situation, or a complete person. The erotic partner of imagination and desire is created or given only in fragments. Like a broken statue the parts of which we find or examine one by one: torso, arms, legs, head, or belly—all separate objects.

But the very same thing happens in the fulfilled eroticism of a sexual act. In darkness the body is split into fragments, into separate objects. They have an independent existence. It is my touch that makes them exist *for me*.

Touch is a limited sense. Unlike sight, it does not embrace the entire person. Touch is invariably fragmentary; it decomposes. A body experienced through touch is never an entity; it is just a sum of fragments that exist side by side. They touch each other but do not grow together. To put it more precisely, they continue to be contingent in relation to each other but do not create a form. They are not a structure.

In darkness the body yields in fragments. I use the term darkness metaphorically. Eroticism always means being pushed into darkness, even if the act takes place in full daylight.

For that matter sight, like touch, becomes a fragmentary sense during the act. It concentrates on a fragment of the body: on the eyes, the mouth, or the forehead, on the nape of the neck, or on the belly. The partner's body yields in a different perspective, from unusual angles, in magnifying close-ups. This is important, as in the case of well-known pictures whose fragments strike us as new and different when photographed in close-up. The fragments of the body embraced by sight during the act of love are, like touch, incoherent and disordered. The eyes open and close; a fragment of the body given in a tight close-up has passed from sight.

I have seen only a few abstract sculptures that manage to recall or transmit something of real eroticism. Though it may sound strange, this sort of thing happens less frequently in painting. The pictures of Max Ernst exude eroticism. I have lately seen a painting by Leonore Fini in which a real sexual act is so obscured and blurred that only its individual fragments pervade the fantasies of imagination. The act is implied, literally and concretely, underneath the picture, under its texture, under the last layer of paint. If films had more imagination, they could show, perhaps, the true eroticism of the tight close-ups of sight and touch.

In the close-up of sight, as on a wide screen, one's own body and the partner's body change their proportions. It is exactly this type of vision, made monstrous by close-up, that can be discerned in some scenes of Gulliver's second travel to the Brobdingnag which have a clearly sexual implication. Swift expressed in them his dislike for women, which was only a part of his general hatred of the bodily aspect of man. The body changes its proportions even more in the literal close-ups, those tight close-ups of touch.

The body seems then to be dissected, as it were, reduced to atoms, pervaded, touched from within. It has its stickiness and dryness, moisture, roughness, and temperature. Touch brings out the muscles and tissues, joints and cartilage. It penetrates to the very skeleton, to the bones, making them emerge from nonexistence, and surrending them up to the senses and to consciousness; one's own consciousness and that of the partner. The fingers get under the skin, as it were. Until now the body within was like a stone; now it begins to exist. Touch becomes a life-giving dissection. But even in this instance touch retains its fragmentary structure and does not create a person, or at least creates one that is altogether different. The erotic "space" of touch is not within the three-dimensional area of sight. It is an area of many senses at once, nearest perhaps to the "spaces" created by taste and smell, much denser than the area of sight. The body becomes a glove turned inside out; it is experienced and perceived from within.

The function of language in eroticism undergoes a change too. Language goes back to its roots, to the moment of its birth. Either it is nonarticulated, a cry and an onomatopoeic sound, as if it were only just learning the names of things and actions. Or it is articulated and then its function is magical, or akin to magic. The difference between a concept and an object, between a token and a thing, is blurred or disappears. Language becomes action, like in magic: it causes a thing or an action to

exist just by naming it and gives it qualities that have been expressed in words. This erotic, or rather suberotic, language
constantly breaks taboos. For taboos last longest in the sphere
of language; they are almost invariably the relics of an era in
which the connections between a thing and its name were
magical.

Eroticism is always an act of cognition. In it the body is being dissected, and senses constantly check on one another. Sight
becomes endowed with some of the functions of touch, and
vice versa. Eroticism is a constant appeal from sight to touch
and from touch to sight; it is as if the existence of one's partner
were constantly being questioned and required constant proof.

A partner created by erotic imagination exists entirely in
those intermingling areas of sight and touch. He is the glove
turned inside out. This applies both to the real partner and to
the imagined one; to the partner of an act fulfilled as to that of
the imagination. This is why Chiaromonte is both right and
wrong.

For in fact it is four persons who go to bed together: the
pair of real lovers and the pair of partners created; two bodies
and two partners of imagination and desire, created mutually
by each other.

Eroticism is testing the partner who has been created by
oneself. In this testing, it is the body that will be the last instance and the final resort. One's own body and that of the
partner. Because one's own body, too, is on the outside; it is
being put to the test and experienced in the same way as that of
the partner. One's own body, too, is an object. One's body is a
medium through which one takes and gives pleasure. Pleasure
can be located, and so one can separate oneself from it.

But the paradox and sadness of eroticism consists in the fact
that its absolute fulfillment is not possible. Testing is possible
only during the act itself. To possess means just that. But the
moment the act is over, the partner and his/her body become

separate again. The body is a stranger again, it exists for itself and not for me. The partner, real and created, the partner of the consummated act and the partner of imagination, becomes ambiguous again. He/she has to be tested again. And testing is possible only through a new act, through another appeal to the body. For the body is an essence and there is no other essence apart from the body. But the reduction to essence is possible only for a fleeting moment. The partner escapes again and cannot be permanently reduced to the body alone.

This is probably the reason for the failure of every passion, and possibly also for the failure of the phenomenon we call love.

Translated by Bolesław Taborski

ALOE

I went yesterday to Roccaraso. On my way I saw aloe trees. They grow wild here, but are not so big as those in Cannes.

When I first became ill, Christine told my wife to give me little bits of aloe three times a day. She brought a pot herself. There were other small pots of aloe in our children's nursery. Three times a day I used to cut off a bit of the thick leaf, clear off its thorns, cut it into little pieces with a knife and put sugar on it. The leaves were thick and had a green, glossy jelly under a thin peel, which I used to remove with a knife. Juice flowed out of the jelly. The aloe salad tasted sweet-sour, like some Chinese dishes. My wife saw to it that I ate aloe three times a day. Christine's husband had a cavity in his lungs as big as a nut, but he ate aloe for three months and the cavity filled in.

Later I was taken to a hospital. Next day my wife brought me a pot of aloe. The hospital director let me have the use of her study, so I had a room to myself. I put the pot of aloe on her desk. Three times a day I cut off a piece of its leaf, two or three inches wide, cut it into little bits and ate it. The aloe was big and well grown, but every day it became more and more like an invalid. Fresh shoots were the tastiest; they had softer peel and were juicier. I cut them in half, from the top. After a week the cut-off leaves of the aloe looked like cut-off hands. I looked at the aloe all day long. The desk stood in front of the bed. The aloe was, after all, the only living creature in the room, myself apart. I got used to it. I could not go on eating it any longer. I felt as if I were committing cannibalism. At that time I found out that the doctors were suspecting something quite different from just TB. I had known about it from the start. I knew and I did not know.

Translated by Bolesław Taborski

A SHORT TREATISE ON DYING

For the last week I have again felt a great urge to smoke, especially in the mornings, when I begin to write, and in the evenings. I gave up smoking more than thirteen months ago. I have my private proof of the existence of original sin and the corruption of human nature. The process of giving up smoking takes at least a year; it is hard, painful, and prolonged. And then—one cigarette is enough to destroy everything and make one go back to smoking. As before.

When I first arrived in the hospital I was still smoking, even more than before maybe. R. treated me to English cigarettes. Every day before lunch he used to bring me a news bulletin that he received from his paper. He was a patient on the same floor, in a general ward, opposite the private room I had been given. He coughed and choked constantly and complained of pain in his chest. Common friends of us both who, after paying him a visit, used to look me up told me he was an old TB patient. He felt better and better—so he said, anyway. He was sent home in my third week at the hospital and died when I was still at the sanatorium. He had had *that*. Another of my hospital acquaintances was transferred to the cancer department while I was

there. He, too, complained about his throat, had had a pneu-
mothorax and bronchoscopy three times. He was glad to go.
They would be able to help him there at last, he said. He was
trying to deceive himself. I knew it. Later I knew even better
how to go about this sort of thing.

I should have accepted certain facts even earlier. But I did
not accept them. I did all I could to find out things, but when I
had done so and was very near the truth, I did all I could to
have it denied. First I wanted everybody to tell me yes, then I
demanded of them repeated denials.

The next day after my arrival I learned I was not in the TB
department, or at any rate patients treated here did not have
open TB. Sister was even surprised they had sent me there, for
I had a cavity. I told Sister I was put there because the director
had given me her room. Sister accepted this.

From the start I feared just that one thing. I calmed down
only when I learned that there was a cavity. I was so afraid of
that other thing that I was not really worried about TB. I could
not even be concerned about it, or take it seriously; never,
neither before nor after the operation when everything cleared
itself up, nor in the sanatorium, nor later in the South. I had
been afraid of that other thing; I relaxed when I learned it was a
cavity. Cavity is not *that*. I was telling everyone I was lucky. It
is true that at first they told me there was a tumor, just above
the cavity. The tumor worried me. I telephoned J. and R.; they
were the most expert TB patients among my friends. I knew
the tumor had to be removed by an operation. I was very much
afraid of the operation. I got used to the idea of going to a sanatorium. I imagined the sanatorium a little like Mann's *Magic
Mountain,* and a little like the University Library. Or at least
like a holiday camp. It would be like a vacation; not a very long
vacation at that. I would read a little, rest a little, something
would be happening. Madame Chauchat would bring small silver pencils. I toyed with the idea of a sanatorium, fascinated.

All this did not last longer than a week, or ten days at most. Ten days after the first X-ray I was already at the hospital in Płocka Street. It happened because of the tumor. I became afraid again. My doctor assured me that cancer never occurred together with TB. And there was a cavity, big as a plum, in the upper right corner of my lung. These cavities have lovely, fruity names. They are called a pea, a bean, a grape, a cherry, a hazelnut, or a walnut.

Opposite the hospital, in a cul-de-sac off Płocka Street, stood an ordinary three-story house. Facing my window was a two-room flat with a big balcony. On the balcony a little girl played all day long. She could not have been more than eight years old; she was tiny and had very fair hair. She was alone all day. She must have been rising very early, because when I went to the window in the morning—and in the hospital morning really means morning—the girl was already on the balcony. Admittedly, I took advantage of my privileged position and took my temperature still asleep, or did not take it at all, and I woke only to eat breakfast, which was often brought to me well after seven. The little girl was already playing with her big doll or taking care of the household. She was very industrious: she washed, cleaned the flat, watered the flowers, scrubbed the floor. She was always alone. Only in the evening, sometimes very late, a young woman came, with a man. Only occasionally in the afternoon there was another girl in the flat, a few years older than she. She must have been attending school or sent somewhere, for I saw her very infrequently.

In my first days at the hospital I used to spend many hours by the window. I was not much inclined to reading. I avoided company: at that time I did not know anybody in the hospital and was afraid of the place. The hospital did not draw me in, or at any rate did so very slowly. As a matter of fact I was excluded from many situations affecting others because of my private room. In the corridors people talked only about diseases.

This was what I feared most. I did not want to be drawn in. All my friends had warned me that I should not let myself be drawn in. At that time I was also bored by that kind of talk.

The hospital still seemed to me a bit unreal. The real life was over there, beyond the windows. I was still over there, outside, rather than in the hospital. All the other patients, however, were here, not over there. That impression remained with me for a long time; for the whole of my stay at the hospital and even later at the sanatorium. A month, or six weeks perhaps; until the time when I went on my first leave. It was then that everything was reversed: I found that I belonged here, not there, outside.

In the sanatorium military discipline was observed and one had to obtain a pass to leave it. I returned in panic and my only wish was to go to bed. I felt safe only in the sanatorium. My friends talked about things I was not interested in. I talked to them about the sanatorium. They listened out of courtesy, then returned to their affairs. I was glad to be at home with my family, but only for a little while. Home—this was something too tiring for me. My wife wanted to tell me all about my daughter. I avoided the subject as best I could. I did not want to know. There was practically nothing I wanted to know. Reality was *there*, not here. I was exempt there from so many things. However, a few days after my return to the sanatorium, I began to long for a pass again. But I knew by now that *there* is *here*, and *here* is *there*. That my real life is the sanatorium.

It was different when people came to visit me. They had to travel for nearly two hours. This was enough to make them adjust themselves to a visit at a sick bed, a visit in a sanatorium. They came only to see me; they came to be with me and "for me." From the outset they were bound by visiting hours. I wanted to prolong these hours, or make my visitors come earlier. I used to accompany them past the gate, and on several occasions I managed to go by car for a cup of coffee or lunch; with or without a pass. Sometimes I used to get out through a gap in the wire netting that surrounded the grounds of the sanatorium.

But the sanatorium and its discipline went on existing; the regulations were infringed by me and by my visitors. The visits were happening in a world to which *I* belonged, not they. The excursions by car to have lunch at Świder were an escape, but an escape from my world. The entire meaning of the escape consisted in the fact that in an hour or two I would return. That was, for that matter, the only thing reminding me of *The Magic Mountain:* the reversal of "here" and "there"; and those returns from leave when I came back, like a frightened animal, in panic, to retire with a feeling of relief to my den; to put a blanket over my head; the blanket every fibre of which was impregnated with the sickly hospital smell.

But all that happened later. During my stay in the hospital I used to spend many hours by the window. In the house opposite nothing particular was happening. Only sometimes a married couple would quarrel. Once or twice a week a man came to the young woman who lived on the first floor; or one of three girls, who also lived there, ran in her nightgown to shut the window. But in fact, only the little girl opposite existed, as far as I was concerned. She went to bed very late. She used to wait for her parents, or rather for her mother; the man, as I found out later, was not her father. Sometimes all of them would sit at a table; often the woman and the man went at once to the other room; on those occasions the woman walked about in her slip for a while, then quickly drew the curtains. The little girl went out on the balcony with a very heavy and rusty watering can and watered the flowers.

For the first few days the little girl did not pay any attention to me; I was just part of the big house opposite. A hospital is like a prison: from below, or from the houses facing it, one sees only prisoners and guards, patients and people in white overalls. Patients and prisoners both look alike from outside. When

I tried to call her, she ran away from the balcony for a little while and hid in her flat. Later she got used to the fact of my being at the window opposite her; in the morning she waved me a greeting with her hand, or the doll she was holding. But she remained cautious to the end and did not want to reply to my questions what her name was.

All this did not last for very long; two weeks at most. Of course, hospital time, like prison time, is quite different from "ordinary" time. Even now, from a year's distance, these two months spent in the hospital seem very long to me; particularly the first two weeks, with the little girl in the window opposite.

Two weeks later I took advantage of the fact that a young woman doctor was on night duty; she used to come quite often and have tea with me in my room. From her I found out everything there was to know. I told her I knew everything from the hospital director anyhow. The young doctor then confirmed that I had *it*. For the next three days I did everything I could to have it proved to me that it was not true. I involved quite a few people in this campaign: my own doctor; the father of one of my students, who was a professor of surgery; Christine—who first brought me the aloe—and two other Christines who worked in the X-ray department. They all called on me and told me it was not true.

After three days I asked for a tranquilizer, the good old concoction of bromide, valerian, and a few other traditional drugs. I drank a bottle of it daily. I had no dreams afterward. I used to drink two tablespoonfuls before putting my book away. Sometimes I fell asleep book in hand.

For a few days after the "night of truth" I kept going up to the window two or three times a day. I waved at the girl and stood there for a quarter of an hour or so. I still looked at her; I was still interested in her activities. Then I went up to the window less and less frequently. Once or twice I did not even bother to get up till lunch time. I shaved only after lunch, before visiting time. The world began to shrink very fast. At the end of a few more days it ceased to exist beyond my window.

I remained in the same room for three more weeks, until the operation. I had to come up to the window, because I had to open and shut it daily, in the morning and in the evening. But I did not see the little girl opposite anymore.

In my first days at the hospital I had told my wife about the girl. A few weeks later my wife asked me about her. I did not know whom she meant. I had forgotten her existence. "Look," said my wife, "she is standing on the balcony doing the washing. Poor child!" I think it was then that I realized for the first time that one cannot survive one's own death.

Translated by Bolesław Taborski

THE SEXUAL TRIANGLE

On the model of Lévi-Strauss's well-known "culinary triangle" one could conceive of a primal triangle with Life on the side of Culture, Death on the side of Nature, and a apex corresponding to Sex and Food, the two mediators between life and death.

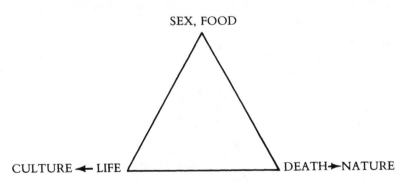

This primordial triangle is the homologue of the sexual triangle, whose vertices correspond to Mouth, Genitals, and Anus, defining a semantic system of relations and oppositions (exchanges, symbolic indentifications, correlations, and inversions) between bodily functions and their linguistic and mythic designations. Corresponding to the fundamental opposition Mouth/Anus are the consecutive analogues of the oppositions voice/noise, breathing/farting, and eating/excreting. "To excrete" is parallel with "to vomit" and is the inverse of "to eat." Corresponding to the opposition Mouth/Anus is the second fundamental opposition—between nourishment and excrement.

In this classification system the idealization of the mouth corresponds to the abasement of the anus: the "hole" is related to the cloaca (meaning both a sewer, a receptacle for filth, and in its zoological use referring to the common orifice of the urinary, eliminatory, and genital systems in vertebrate embryos), to filth, and, in the semantics of myths, to the "gates of Hell." According to this system "to spit," the inverse of "to drink," would be the consecutive of "to shit." "Eat shit" is consecutive and parallel, at the symbolic level, to "Go to hell!" The verb of exchange between Mouth and Anus is always, significantly, "to eat" with its parallels and inversions. The exchange of food against excrement both unites and puts in opposition all the signs of Mouth and Anus (*la bouche d'égout*) and becomes the paradigm generating all the permutations of "to eat" in social relations (e.g., in dirty jokes) and in myths.

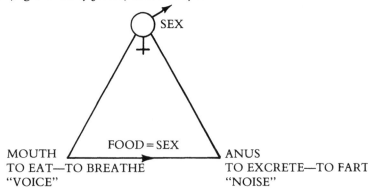

At the stage of infantile erotism sexual curiosity is oriented toward the anus, and nourishment symbolically identified with sex (food = sex). With sexual maturity the two terms of this linguistic and symbolic equation are reversed (sex = food). In the linguistic system of English the verb of transition between Mouth and Genitals is again "to eat," with its parallel "to suck."[1] In the system of French the sign of the exchange between "la Bouche" and "la Sexe" is "baiser" (to kiss/to copulate). This anatomical identification is already found in Latin, with "labia." The fear of castration is often symbolized by the devouring mouth of the "vagina dentata." Sexual "nourishment" is signified by "la chair" (flesh, meat) and most markedly by "la consommation du marriage." In English, sexual "nourishment" is symbolized by "meat" (e.g., "meat market"). Another symbolic identification is manifested in the use of "head" for the male as well as the female sex. As in *Romeo and Juliet*:

> SAMPSON: I will be cruel with the maids and cut off their heads.
>
> GREGORY: The heads of the maids?
>
> (1.1.26–29)

In Shakespeare's *Measure for Measure* this exchange is decisive for the structure of the work:

> PROVOST: Can you cut off a man's head?
>
> POMPEY: If the man be a bachelor, sir, I can: but if he be a married man, he's his wife's head, and I can never cut off a woman's head.
>
> (4.2.1–4)

In the system of physiological language of the Trobrianders, the eyes, as Malinowski noted, are the seat of sexual desire: "magila kayta," literally the "eyeball," is the summit of the entire system.[2]

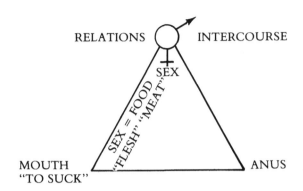

The expressions for coitus at the vertex of Sex have a characteristic signification: "intercourse" *(le rapport)*, consort *(le commerce)*, and so on. Equivalently, coitus can be signified within the paradigms of spacial models as "flying," "climax" *(le comble)*, "coming" *(jouir)*. In the advertisement for an American airline, the stewardess's invitation to passengers to "Fly me!" has blatant sexual connotations.

In the English of the sixteenth to the nineteenth centuries one could use in place of "coming" another verb, "dying" *(mourir)*. In Shakespeare and in the poems of Donne "dying" was used as well as "coming." In *Romeo and Juliet* the last words of Juliet are "Romeo, I come! This do I drink to thee" (4.4.58). To "come" here has the hidden meaning to "die."

In classical French there is the same exchange between the vertices of the Genitals and of the Anus in the symbolic connection of "la petite mort" (orgasm) and "la mort" (death).

In nineteenth-century English, in the age of Victorian repression, the place of "coming" was filled by the term "spending," with the sexual discharge equated with money (e.g., the expression "to spend a penny"). And in most semiotic systems "spending" is consecutive to and parallel with "excreting." The descent from Genitals to Anus in the sexual triangle is heavily stigmatized: it is the way of renunciation and repression. It is also the locus of taboos.

The vertex of the Anus, on the side of Nature, is the paradigm of Death, of Dirt, of Hell. The Hole is at the same time animal and monster.

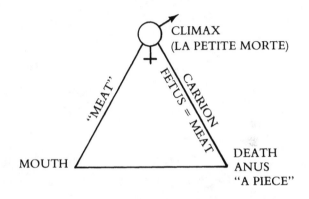

The sign of exchange between the vertices of the Genitals and the Anus is again "baiser" ("baise mon cul") or "foutre" in its two senses: "fous-moi le cul" (fuck my ass) and "je suis foutu" (I'm fucked up). Through the identification of the female with the ass the semiotic system reflects male domination: a "good piece of ass" is finally just a "good piece."

"Meat" also signifies the corpse in Shakespeare—flesh is transformed into carrion. This symbolism of food is repeated again in the parallelism of the signifier through which fetus = meat. In mythic semantics menstruation and childbirth are often represented by vomiting, the inverse and correlative of both eating and excreting.

The sexual triangle delimits a semantic field, but from the *outside,* on the surface of the enunciation, in the semantics of concrete, visible, social signs. But in the interior of this triangle, at the profound existential level, one can construct another triangle whose vertices would be "I," "You/the Other," and the depersonalized third-person "It" (*Ça*).

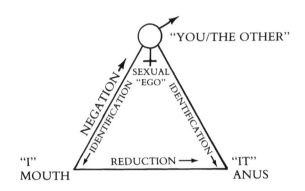

"I"-Mouth receives its sexual denomination in its relation with "You/the Other"; "You/the Other" for "I"-Mouth is the Genitals—either penis or vagina. On the other hand, "It" is not neuter like the Latin "id" but is the residuum for libido—male, female, or bisexual. Jung's archetypes *animus* and *anima,* which in some way replaced the Freudian "it," have a gender: *animus* is the unconscious of woman and *anima* of man.

The Other for "I"-Mouth is also one's own sex, one's own genitals. At the level of linguistic signs the penis is often called by the proper name of its possessor, for example, "Peter" *(le petit Pierre),* and similarly the vagina called, for example, *la petite Sophie.* In Polish the popular diminutives of female names are often employed in place of the generic name of the vagina (Zoska, Marysia). In French slang *fleur-de-Marie* means virginity. In English the names chosen for the female genitals are common female names, "Mary Jane" or "Fanny."

At the profound level, at the level, if you will, of the Unconscious, there are two fundamental and contradictory relations between Mouth and Genitals, between "I" and "You/the Other," symbolic identity and symbolic negation:

Relations of symbolic identity
a. identity of "I"-Mouth with one's own genitals.

    b. transfigured identity (displacement) of "I"-Mouth met-
amorphosed into the opposite sign: "I"-a male with vagina; "I"-a female with penis.

    c. identity of "You/the Other" with one's own genitals.

    d. symbolic identity of "You/the Other" with the oppo-
site sex.

(The system of the French language seems exceptional
in giving the masculine gender to "vagina" *(le vagin)* and the
feminine gender to most of the names for the male genitals.
Thus the paradox of cursing a man "Tu es con" is really
symptomatic.)

    Relations of symbolic negation

    a. utter negation of its sexual Other by "I"-Mouth.

    b. complete negation of the sex of "You/the Other" by
"I"-Mouth.

In certain works of Freud *(On the Mechanism of Paranoia,*
1911; *Repression,* 1915; *The Loss of Reality in Neuroses and Psy-
choses,* 1925) "vicissitudes and deviations" are often ana-
lyzed—one could say in anticipation of structuralism—as permutations of signs in a symbolic algebra. Inversion is, already
in 1915 (long before Merleau-Ponty), shown by Freud to be
the displacement of the Look and of the Object of the Look:

    a. The subject regards   = The subject's sex beneath
        his/her own sex   the gaze of the subject

    b. The subject regards   c. The subject's sex as
        his/her own sex as an   beneath the gaze of the
        alien object   Other
        (voyeurism)   (exhibitionism)

In our triangular schema, exhibitionism is the sex of "Me-
as-Other" which looks at/articulates the Mouth. In voyeurism
it is the sex of "You/the Other" which looks at/articulates the
"I"-Mouth. As in Freud the projections of the libido can be

presented as transformations of discourse (cf. Freud's presentation of the transformations of the basic homosexual wish underlying paranoia—"I [a man] *love him*"—in *On the Mechanism of Paranoia*). Delirium, then, is the profound displacement of the three vertices of our sexual triangle, with the reversal of its relations.

Repression, or existential denial, is the symbolic identification of the vertex of "You/the Other" with that of the "It." The Anus isn't marked for sex. "You" (masculine or feminine) reduced to the Hole, to "It," is degraded and depersonalized. Among the Trobrianders the most serious insult is "ikaye pwala," literally, "he screws shit" (Malinowski). The reduction of "I"-Mouth to the Anus is at the same time correlative and opposed to the reduction of "You/the Other" to the Hole. According to Freud, the first identification reflects masochistic tendencies, the second, sadistic tendencies.

The deep structure of the sexual triangle doesn't translate itself directly through linguistic signs, but nevertheless the signs are encoded there. The operational value of the triangle is in grasping relations and permutations, but it is not merely a diagram. I believe one can use it for the classification of signs, for example, in rites of passage, where "I"-Mouth must identify itself, through symbolic signs, with its own genitals and with the sex of the Other in becoming aware of the "It": the Hole and Death. I believe also that the juxtaposition of the linguistic surface and of symbolic activity can define and direct the decoding of clinical and poetic delirium.

If we divide the triangles, primordial, sexual, and existential, by a vertical axis dividing the apex of Sex/the Other, the fields of Eros and Thanatos emerge—the first oriented toward the side of culture, the second toward the side of nature. The zone of taboo and sexual repression also emerges. The triangles indicate, then, a semiotic universe of existence in its corporeal limits. In the last analysis the vertices represent "to be," "to be-coming," "to be-dying" *(etre, etre-jouir, etre-mourir)*.

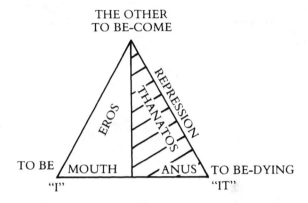

THE OTHER
TO BE-COME

EROS

REPRESSION

THANATOS

TO BE / MOUTH | ANUS \ TO BE-DYING
"I"   "IT"

Notes

1. In *The Language of Sexuality* (Jefferson, N.C.: McFarland, 1987), Alan Richter writes: "What is interesting, however, is the annexing especially of food and eating terms to sexual terminology. There must be strong parallels between eating and sex if one can take language from another; the mixing of metaphors must imply a strong common viewpoint" (p. 19). In his glossary Richter includes "meat," "flesh" as food, "a bit of fish" (obsolete), "taking a slice," "bit on a fork," "have a nibble," "taste," "pudding" (intercourse), "appetite" (often in Shakespeare), and "jelly," "cream," "milk," "honey," "salt," "saucy."

2. According to Richter's glossary, in the sixteenth–seventeenth centuries "eye" was a euphemism or metaphor for "vagina." In French from the eighteenth century *oeil* (eye) has the idiomatic meaning of "ass" (Pierre Guirard, *Dictionnaire érotique* [Paris, 1978]). Bataille's most obsessive sexual novel is entitled *L'oeil*.

Translated by Mark Rosenzweig

IN THE KITCHEN OF
A SHAMANESS

For Carlo Ginzburg

I t was all quite ordinary. But what amazed me was the
number of brooms. They were stuck in the fence with the
bristles sticking up like straw scarecrows at the gate and
along the hall by the entrance to the kitchen, one after the other
lined up against the wall, little ones and big ones reaching almost up to the ceiling. That was ten or perhaps even twelve
years ago, in Seoul during the Congress of Third World Theaters, or of the Third Theater, as it was later to be known. On
the first day of the congress, a friend of mine, a French anthro-
pologist, told me that there were still practicing shamans in Ko-
rea. Similar to the Siberian shamans of a bygone era. But the
Korean shamans are mostly women. Late in the evening we
were taken to see one of those woman shamans, supposedly the
most powerful of all. It must have been at least a hundred kilo-
meters from Seoul, because we drove for almost three hours,
but the last part of the trip was along back roads.

In the darkness it all looked like the Polish countryside.
Dogs were barking, the house, or rather the dumpy little farm-
house, was located on the outskirts of the village. A wide door

led from the kitchen to the main room. It was a large room, with benches set in front of the tables. It was already almost full. The people must have come from some distance, because almost all of them had huge bundles that they put down beside them or kept slung over their shoulders. The women came with their children. With their kerchiefs pulled down over their heads, they could just as well have been Polish peasant women. The woman of the house put in front of each of us a small plate with honey and a larger plate with grain. "That's her," our guide informed us. She too looked like an ordinary country-woman, except she was a head taller than the rest; she wore a kerchief and what seemed to be several layers of skirts, since one was sticking out from under the other. Her black hair was plaited in two long, heavy braids. She must have been quite attractive in her prime, but she couldn't have been very young anymore because her daughter, who limped and would succeed her as shamaness, was already worn and wrinkled.

Both the mother and daughter began to wash the kitchen floor. It was a furious scrubbing. They tucked up their skirts and through the open door we could see their big red thighs. They must have dumped pails of hot water on the floor, because steam was pouring through the door and for a short while fogged up the entire room. They must have opened the door to the courtyard then, because a flock of clucking hens burst into the kitchen and started to peck at the scattered grain. Two white roosters flapped their wings in the air.

It was just then that it started. But I am at a loss to say exactly how. Suddenly the room became dark with heavy smoke from some burning herbs. But it's also possible that a torch was lighted, because it grew bright in the kitchen. Then I was admitted to the kitchen, along with three or four other foreigners. The lame daughter was beating with all her strength on two pails turned upside down and a huge kettle. She was drumming with whatever came within her reach: first with a wooden spoon, and after it broke, with the handle of a spade. The shamaness started to dance. At first it wasn't a dance at all. Her whole body simply started to shake all over, each part as it were independently, first her braids, then her loose, colorful blouse with the brilliant buttons began to "dance" on her as though her enormous breasts had split her bra. And then her belly, with her skirts rising up and then floating down. Then all of a sudden, still in place, with her arms upraised like the wings of a heavy bird just before taking off, she began to whirl like a top. It was a strange twirling, at times it seemed that she had sprung into the air.

Then abruptly she stopped, her blouse and skirts still swinging. The drumming of her lame daughter became deafening. "Now she is going to call forth the spirits," explained our translator. The shamaness began to draw out of herself strange squealing sounds that seemed to issue from her belly, perhaps even from lower down, from her womb itself. There followed some incantations. "She is speaking in tongues," whispered our guide from the theater in Seoul. And he turned pale. "She is summoning the dead," he continued. "Now she is calling the Spirit of the North Wind—in Russian." But it wasn't in Russian. And only a white rabbit came into the kitchen through the open door.

The herbs were being burned again, and everyone started to choke. Now a trio of women, the daughter and two other young ones, started beating as though demented on whatever and with whatever they could lay their hands on. The whole kitchen went berserk. Everything began jumping up and down: pots on the stove, mugs on the shelves, plates, forks, knives. The shamaness was now dancing about the room: from wall to wall, around the stove and from the door to the window so that it seemed at times as if she had flown out and then, rebuffed by alien powers, flown back in. Whereupon she collapsed on the floor.

The kettle beating stopped. It was absolutely silent. Only the children could be heard crying. But this sudden silence was as earsplitting as the thundering percussion had been before. At that point several old crones began to slip into the kitchen. One after the other. Six or seven of them. All clad in black and in black stockings, the kind southern European women wear on Sunday outings. But their stockings were hanging loosely on their wizened, crooked legs. They lifted the shamaness from the floor; she was still rigid; they propped her like a huge puppet taller by two heads than any of them; and they tossed her back and forth slowly like the Russian toy *vanka-vstanka*. After a while, they started to dance, holding her still-inert body erect. In total silence. And suddenly they started to make faces. Frightening grimaces. They opened toothless mouths, clicked their tongues, chuckled, tilted their heads on pitifully thin necks like molted herons, jostled one another, and slapped their buttocks. The lame daughter began beating the kettle again. Finally the shamaness came out of her rigid state. She began to whirl along with the old crones, sticking her hands under their skirts and tearing their blouses off their breasts. The daughter kept beating faster and faster on the kettle with some kind of wooden rolling pin. Above this whirling mass of bodies, various rags could be seen flying in the air, and then suddenly someone's skirt went sailing up to the ceiling. The daughter stopped beating on the pails. One after the other, the old women fell flat on the stone floor, like huge squashed frogs, except that their feet, sticking out from under their skirts, twitched for a few moments and their fingers contracted and opened like at the last moment of an orgasm.

We left the kitchen and returned to the main room. The kerosene lamps had been extinguished. It was nearly daybreak. The daughter brought a tray of hot bread cakes. They must have just been taken off the oven's hot iron plate. The shamaness started to distribute mugs of piping hot green tea. She was wearing the same kerchief, her layered skirts were now in per-fect order. Everything became ordinary again. She was simply entertaining her guests as any peasant woman would do.

Through the door we could see the old women getting up off the kitchen floor. They were straightening their skirts, but-toning up their blouses, tying their kerchiefs around their heads. Then they went to the hall and picked up their brooms. One af-ter the other, with these huge brooms, they began to sweep first the kitchen floor, then the hall, and finally, taking longer, along the doorstep and out into the courtyard. And it was at that very moment, in the kitchen of a shamaness in a Korean village, that it all became familiar to me. As though something once known and long forgotten suddenly came back. Like the midnight scene in Wyspiański's *Wedding,* when the young Isia still in her night-gown chases the Mulch out and sweeps the bits of flax and hemp out of the room after him. As in the last scene of *A Midsummer Night's Dream,* when Puck sweeps the stage after all the dreams are over: "I am sent with broom before, / To sweep the dust be-hind the door." Like the children with huge brooms that Goethe remembered at daybreak after St. John's Night, sweeping the streets clean of the still-smoldering ashes. The Sabbath was over. Or perhaps it had only been dreamed. The old women were still bent over their brooms.

The same evening, back in Seoul, I attended a performance of an avant-garde Japanese group. The faces of the actors were painted red, and black and red as in the traditional Kabuki. But the painting covered only the lower half of their faces. That performance of third-world theater was half-Artaud. At times this joining of two cruelties—of East and West—was arresting. But for me, that night in the shamaness's kitchen was more ar-resting than all the theaters of the first, second, and third worlds.

Translated by Jadwiga Kosicka

THE HEART ATTACK

For Dr. Halina Kotlicka

I

We all know the world shrinks when we leave childhood. Łazienki Park in Warsaw is still full of secrets and impossible for me to cross. I was left alone there as a child and lost my way chasing a boy in a sailor suit on a tricycle. I ran after him along a path and then found myself stranded in front of a satyr with a chipped nose. The world, shrunken and tamed once childhood is left behind, stretches again when old age begins. It expands vertically, though, not horizontally. What was level is no longer level. Flat suddenly becomes steep. Houses without elevators suddenly acquire stories they never had. Quaker Path, the street where I live in Stony Brook, seemed flat as a board for ten years. But walking back from campus two years ago, I was carrying a heavy briefcase that never weighed much before and, midway home, I noticed that my street rises to a hill. Halfway up, I had to stop and put down the briefcase.

99

2

The pain was dull. It was really quite mild, but there was something strange about it. It started at the breastbone but did not end anywhere. The pain was mild, but it was all over the body. I felt I had to lie down immediately. I was having dinner at the Journalists Club during my visit to Warsaw, and I asked to be taken back to the apartment on Nabielak Street. I did not finish my coffee and I put out a half-smoked cigarette. It was not until a week later when I craved nicotine once again that I remembered the half-smoked cigarette, felt it in my throat, and regretted leaving it.

Back in my room, I lay down but the pain persisted. It was still mild, but, curiously, I did not feel like getting up or even talking. I had a party to attend that afternoon. First, I sent a message that I would be late, then that I would not come at all. I was supposed to leave for Cracow at six the following morning. Otherwise, I would never have called Dr. K. "Strange pains," I said.

An ambulance arrived half an hour later. They carried me out on a stretcher. Quite a ritual, I thought. They asked in the emergency room on Stepińska Street if I could walk to the electrocardiograph unit. The question seemed ridiculous; it was only thirty or forty steps. I went back to the waiting room on my own. A moment later, the doctor on duty came and said it was a heart attack. So, I would not be leaving for Cracow. I called Irena and asked her to inform friends I would not be coming and that it was a heart attack. "Where are you? Are you in the ICU?" I did not yet know what the ICU (intensive care unit) was, but her voice told me something had happened. To me. I realized I should call K. at once. "Let me talk to the doctor," K. ordered. She must have yelled at him terribly. I heard in the depths of my body that I was to lie down immediately and that she was sending an ambulance. And only when I was again lying on a stretcher did it finally hit me: I was having a heart attack. Up until then, it was always others who had heart attacks. All I knew about heart attacks is that one dies of them.

3

The pain was still dull, only it seemed to be everywhere. Or, rather, it was as if I were beyond this pain. I felt I was walking away, leaving myself and the pain behind just as one can leave oneself for a moment while on marijuana and, with some effort, simply go away. And, like with marijuana, time slows and feels different inside. Inside me, the same pain persisted. I do not know how long I waited for an ambulance, an hour or a day.

I held someone's hand in the ambulance, probably one of the nurses from Miedzylesie. I was not scared. Later, I remembered that I had asked her not to be scared and insisted I was merely pretending to be in pain and that none of this was real. But it really hurt when they put the IV in my arm. The needle was inserted into the vein of my right wrist, which had been immobilized. Perhaps the veins were too frail or too narrow. It seemed as though needles were constantly being inserted and withdrawn.

I knew I was being saved. Three or four heads hovered around me, and I felt myself laid out like in an exhausting dream. The right hand, which seemed detached as though it were severed, was connected to an IV, the chief source of pain. The left hand was taped and bound to measure the pulse. My lips, pressed to a rubber oxygen tube, also seemed detached. I was still not scared. I must have lost and regained consciousness several times (not until three in the morning was I left alone even for a moment, I was later told), but I remember only the sting of needles and the nearness of eyes during those many hours of alien time. I knew I was drifting away. I remember someone saying, "You're not going to drift off again, not to-day." But who said that and when? I wanted very badly to drift off and for the pain in my right hand to cease. And I thought to myself, I am drifting away so cleanly, without blood, without suffocation. I am only discarding this pain that is so lightly left behind. I am drifting away in whiteness.

4

"You were pretty far gone last night," said the nurse as she brought a water basin the next morning. "That was quite a ruckus you made," the patient next to me added. I could not answer, as the oxygen tube was still taped to my mouth. I could not sit up, either, for soft tubes were coiled all around me like snake skins. Later, I discovered the tubes were attached to five metal disks on my chest.

So this was the ICU. I was in the recovery room of the Railroad Union Hospital in Miedzylesie. There were two other patients in the same room, one across from me and the other to my left; both had suffered heart attacks. This was the morning after the attack. After *my* attack. A heart attack always has its day and hour, its beginning and end. By itself, it is brief. One lives either in the time before the heart attack or in the time after.

Because of its brevity, dying of a heart attack is not like dying of cancer. This is true for the patient and to some extent for his family and friends. By dying, I do not mean the progress of a disease, the body's struggle with an enemy. I mean the fear and dread of death felt by the patient and those closest to him. In my experience, dying was drifting. For other heart attack patients, dying is a piercing pain in the chest. For family and friends, a heart attack is a series of late-night calls to a doctor on duty. For the family and the victim, the dramaturgy of a heart attack is accelerated.

Dying from cancer takes weeks, months, sometimes years. It begins long before diagnosis and often continues even after the verdict has been reversed and the tumor is pronounced benign. I experienced an agony of expectation when I underwent surgery nearly twenty years ago for the removal of what appeared in an X-ray as a dark stain the size of a walnut on the upper lobe of my right lung. For weeks, I watched the fear in the eyes of my wife.

The experience of a heart attack is different. Once the attack is over, one is cured. Of course, another attack is possible and so is a second, a third, or a fourth. But the prognosis of death has nevertheless a different character with coronary disease than with cancer. And not only does it have a different character but—I don't know how else to put it—it has a different metaphysic. Five years of remission is considered a cure for cancer. Yet one continues to die from the incurable fear of a relapse. Dying from cancer, whether slow or rapid, is continuous and gradual and always without respite. Cancer, the terminal disease, is a suspended death sentence. Dying is the suspension of death. The dread of cancer, described in Susan Sontag's moving *Illness as Metaphor,* is this intransgressible *terminus ad quem* that gives the disease the horrifying shape of a verdict, or destiny, *fatum,* as if the work of dark forces. A heart attack has no *terminus* and there are no dark forces. There is only a heart that has failed.

The heart is a sack that pumps blood. The blood from the veins enters the heart through the auricles and is then expelled through the arteries and the aorta. An attack is a wound to the heart. A part of the coronary muscle atrophies and blocks the passage of blood. An attack means atrophy in the heart, the heart's partial death if one survives and complete death if one does not. A wound to the heart heals like all wounds, and, like all wounds, it leaves a scar. A trace remains until death. The ECG is the most exact record of the heart's wounds. It is a graphic image of the attack, the underside of a wave, a valley instead of a peak among a mass of trajectories on cardiographic paper. The lines on our fingertips do not change from birth to death, and they are the only infallible record of our identity. The broken lines of an electrocardiogram, forming hills and valleys, chronicle the history of a heart.

5

When I lifted my head, I saw a box about the size of a small television set above the bed of the patient across from me. A sharp light like a needle relayed a continuously pulsating message from the electrocardiograph to his screen. Once I was able to prop myself up in bed, I discovered that the five metal amplifiers on my chest were sending messages to an identical luminous screen above me. On my third or fourth day in the ICU, Halina Mikołajska visited me. When I sat up to embrace her, she froze. She was not looking at me, she was staring at the screen. I remembered her in many roles, frozen on stage with her wide, almost transparent doe eyes—a Pallas Athena with a small silver-haired head, incomparably suspended on a long and fragile neck. I had never seen her on stage so transfixed with horror. When I moved to greet her, two disks on my chest had slipped. The iridescent notation on the green screen stopped vibrating and stretched out into a broad flat stripe. The nurse on duty instantly rushed to my bedside. The flat line signifies the cessation of the heart—or fallen disks. The nurse reattached the disks. Many weeks later, Halina told me that the flat line on the screen above my tousled hair had recurred in her dreams. And I remembered these lines from Adam Mickiewicz:

> But look, oh, look upon his heart
> Like a scarlet ribbon hung
> Or corals on a necklace strung.

A bleeding stripe there takes its start
And stretches down from breast to feet.
(trans. M. B. Peacock)

As I gained strength, I would sit up from the pillows and gaze intently at the screen into my beating heart. With each vigorous movement, the luminous lines jumped as though startled.

"See how my heart beats," L. would say, placing my hand on her breast. "See how my heart beats," I said and put her hand on my chest. "Look! Only our fingers can see the heart beating beneath warm and naked flesh." I saw for the first time the graph of a beating heart.

The third week I was allowed to walk around, and I slipped off to the nurses' observation room at night. Luminous zigzags beamed from eight little screens above an enormous table. Every patient in the recovery room has his heart plugged to one of those screens. If I had not been chased out, I would have gazed into those beating hearts for hours. Each heart beat differently, forming jagged or blunt teeth as though traced by the fine stitching of a sewing machine or by the sweeping strokes of a pen. But all the hearts were pulsating and their luminous signals fascinated me. I was spying on other people's hearts in the night. There was something disturbingly erotic in this experience, as though the heart's pulse during those hospital nights had become the pulse of sex.

6

A hospital always exists in a separate time and a separate place. But the separation in time and place is even more marked during the weeks of immobilization in the intensive care unit. Sartre wrote that Faulkner's characters and events escape into the past like the landscape and road viewed through the rear window of a car. They are at once already in the past. Before they are, they already were.

In our healthy life, we move through time like passengers on an escalator. While we remain stationary, everything around us imperceptibly shifts into what has been. Others grow older. We age only in the mirror and in other people's eyes. In a healthy life, time is continuous, recorded on a watch or calendar, passing outside us but never through us. The past is yesterday, the future tomorrow, and yesterday and tomorrow belong to the same continuum. Not only does a heart attack have its hour of day or night, but it is a cutting and severance of time. The Before, the pre-attack, is separated from the After, the post-attack.

Only the Before is present during the weeks of immobilization, and the cut is perceived with exceptional sharpness. Immobilization is this distinct time and place, hollow in itself, where the After, the *post*-attack, is a desperate, almost maniacal wish to repeat the *pre*-attack. Continuity of time and sequence is violated, if not destroyed. In more technical or fanciful terms, the diachrony of events is broken, and the pre-attack is contained within synchronic memory while the entire future is a projection of the past, as in Beckett's *Happy Days* or perhaps more clearly in *Krapp's Last Tape*. The sensation of time is a sensation of destruction within time, and hence the dramatic analogies to the experience of a heart attack. Hospital time is filled with boredom, like almost everything that happens on stage in Chekhov. The real drama occurs offstage; on stage, characters talk only about what has been—like patients in hospital beds—but even so, in talking about what has been, the future tense is used. All these analogies are only partially helpful in describing the post-attack experience of survival. Nevertheless, what is important in these analogies is the theatrical dramatization of time.

Someone's last work, painting, or musical score is read simultaneously in two distinct configurations: as simply the latest work in the bio-bibliographical chronology in the regular course of succession, and also as the last work before the author's death in terms of the phenomenology of the end. The last work is never intended as such but sometimes, as in Barthes's *Camera Lucida*, consciousness of imminent death seems to infuse the writing. The phenomenology of the end means that death transforms the final work into the last will and testament. Probably the most egregious misreadings of Shakespeare's *Tempest* were launched on this basis. Yet that is exactly how the last events before the heart attack, the last landscapes and people, those accidental affinities preceding the moment when time is severed, are transformed into elective ones. Accident becomes fate: *fate* in the Hegelian sense. We encounter our own fate as if it belonged to someone else. An enemy. A deadly enemy. The metaphor is literal; the enemy is death.

A week before the attack, I spent a few days in Cracow. On my last evening, I saw Wajda's *Hamlet* at the Wawel, the palace of Polish kings. We waited in front of the upper gate to the courtyard that June night until almost eleven. People tossed garlands into the Vistula—a traditional rite for Wanda, the legendary princess of Cracow. Enormous spires of fireworks erupted like in a dream. It was as cold as in the real Elsinore. We sat in the courtyard, wrapped in blankets and coats, warming each other's hands. A Hamlet from Wyspiański's vision paced through the galleries with a book in his hand. Gertrude was thoroughly prescient. She knew every stone of the Wawel. Ophelia also divined everything but what could she do? She was an ugly old maid. Hamlet mocked her but he was the first man to desire her.

Like Wanda, she threw herself into the Vistula that night. These were only the bare elements of the tragedy. The walls also performed, rising up in the light and falling away into darkness. They were impenetrable. *Hamlet,* normally confined within artificial canvas drops, was carved out of the impenetrability of those walls. I left the theater with T. through deserted public gardens. It was my first night walk through Cracow in seventeen or eighteen years. The last walk had been with W. a year or two before I moved away. I walked together with him once again in Rome a few months before his death. On Via Gulia, we promised each other another long night walk through Cracow from church to church, bar to bar, from the Market to the Piłsudski Mound. This time, I was to return to Cracow within a week. I did not return. I had a ticket for the 6:00 A.M. express. The night before, I had the heart attack.

The third day in the hospital, I asked for Proust's *Albertine disparue* and *Tristan and Isolde.* Initially, I could read no more than a few pages a day. But for the first time, I read Proust as if it were my own history. Albertine was gone. Everything before the attack suddenly took on significance. The irreversible had occurred. Until then, it seemed tomorrow would always be like yesterday. Albertine would come for the evening caresses as Marcel's mother came with goodnight kisses. Then Albertine crashed into a tree and was gone forever. I wept when I read of Albertine's death. For the first time since childhood, I was crying over a book. I was crying for myself. My mother had died. I had lost Albertine.

I had read Proust three times before: twice from beginning to end and once haphazardly. But in the intensive care unit in a hospital bed under a screen of my own beating heart, I read Proust differently. I did not need a madeleine to recover things past. With the pre-attack still in me, I read Proust not to recall past time but to search for a way to repeat the unrepeatable. It was a search for a way to live when the pre-attack, the imperfect, had become the past perfect during the post-attack. *Plusquamperfectum.*

The *Hamlet* at the Wawel was one of the scores of *Hamlets* I have seen; the walk through the empty public gardens and the conversation with T.—one among many walks and one among many conversations. I knew I could return in a week and once again cross the park at night. But as I lay post-attack in my hospital bed in Miedzylesie, *Hamlet* of a week ago became the last *Hamlet* and the walk through the public gardens, the last walk. And if I ever see *Hamlet* again or walk from the Wawel across the public gardens, it will be my first *Hamlet* and my first walk. Like death, or even its shadow, a heart attack endows people and events from the Before, the pre-attack, with symbolic meanings and signs of necessity. That night walk through the public gardens in Cracow was not simply my last walk, it was my only walk.

After Albertine's death, I put Proust aside and read *Tristan and Isolde*. King Mark sends the faithful Tristan over the sea to bring Isolde back to be his wife. On the ship Tristan and Isolde share a bed, separated by a sword. One evening as a storm approaches, Isolde's maid brings golden goblets containing a love potion. Tristan and Isolde transgress the sword that night and sleep together as man and wife. Later, Isolde marries King Mark, and Tristan is exiled. But perhaps the real story is quite different. Tristan and Isolde lay a sword between them but they are lovers from the first night. As the ship approaches the shore where the impatient king is waiting, they suddenly realize what they have done. Overcome with shame, they demand the potion of eternal love from Brangane. This is how the fornicators become tragic lovers and enter the legend.

"My heart, my physical heart, / Is the object of medical inquiry," Władyslaw Broniewski wrote in what is probably his most personal lyrical poem. "My heart, my aching heart, / Is the object of sorrow, / There is one person too few in this empty room." The underside of the wave on the rising and falling lines of the electrocardiogram is the sign of a wound to the heart until death, even after it has healed. But the heart has still another memory and bears still other scars. A heart attack, like perhaps every brush with death, activates this memory.

David, my young friend, the son of friends and my son's high school classmate, wrote to me from a hospital in Jerusalem where he lay waiting to have an operation on a cancerous tumor: "I found out about your illness last night. As you know, I am in pretty much the same predicament and so I can identify with you, though no one can know for sure what the threat of death means to another person. I know most people think that in such situations all you are concerned with is death, and the fear of pain and dying, but that's not the case for me. I have been feeling everything much more intensely and life seems like an incredible thrill, both in the abstract and in the concrete. Perhaps you too feel the same way."

There was always an intensity in David's life. Death does not protect against love, nor love against death. Albertine is always gone when she is present. There is only dying in love and one's own death. That is how I read Proust in intensive care at the hospital in Miedzylesie.

7

"Be careful, it's fragile," said Teresa. I called her Clairvoyant because she worked in the X-ray department. "Your heart is like china." It was not necessary to tell me to be careful. I felt as if the thing inside me were about to shatter, particularly when I was "mobilized" after two weeks. The first time out of bed is almost a ritual. The doctor leads you by the hand as the other patients watch from their beds. He releases you. The bed and the window are very far apart. The thing inside beats. Your hand is taped. The doctor meticulously measures your pulse.

I received twenty tablets of nitroglycerin, "nitros," in a tiny vial on the first day. There are some on every nightstand. When the pain hits, you quickly place a tablet under your tongue, the blood vessels expand and the fear passes. Heart patients never go anywhere without their "nitros," carried like life preservers in the breast pocket. I received a small furry purse for my "nitros" in the sanatorium, and I still carry it today like a fetish.

You carry "nitros" because you carry your heart. After the attack, the heart is constantly present. Although it is in you, it is a thing apart. You listen to it as though it belonged to someone else. But it is yours. It trembles. You feel a cramp. "Doctor, my heart hurt last night."

It was then that I realized I feel inside me everything language says about the heart. I am lighthearted, fainthearted, or heavyhearted. My heart leaps and it can turn to stone. What it means to break someone's heart. Or to strike a blow to the heart. "I am pained at my very heart"—Jeremiah 4:19—"my heart maketh a noise in me; I cannot hold my peace."

8

Small posters with the caption "Save the Heart" hang in the entrance hall and on all three floors of the Railroad Union Sanatorium in Nałeczów. The red heart on them is perfectly symmetrical. But an aorta and pulmonary artery copied from an anatomical atlas unexpectedly protrude from the beautiful symbolic hearts pictured on these posters at the sanatorium for heart patients. The mild Nałeczów lies at the bottom of a steep valley. It has a microclimate with damp mornings and evenings, and nights that are chilly even during heat spells. There are hardly ever storms. Five sanatoriums for heart patients are located in Nałeczów. Each is shown on the town map posted at the main intersection near the bus station and the small marketplace where only apples are sold. The sign above the map reads, "Nałeczów heals the heart." Hearts have been carved with jackknives and nail files into the map and the wooden pole that supports it. They are not perfectly symmetrical like the poster hearts at the sanatorium. They are crooked like the ones on school desks or benches in Łazienki Park. These hearts have faded letters around them and are sometimes pierced by arrows.

On the last day before my departure from Nałeczów, I noticed a couple at the bus stop. The man, whom I had seen before, was probably the oldest patient at the sanatorium: a serious heart operation awaited him. The woman was tanned; she must have spent her vacation in the mountains. Now she stood on the steps of a bus about to leave for Kazimierz. She was dressed all in white and there was something sad about her face. The old man put his hand to his heart without saying a word. His eyes were fixed on the woman until the bus left.

Translated by Michael and Tara Kott

THE MEMORY OF
THE BODY

There is also a sun in the night.

—*Nietzsche, Zarathustra*

The death of which I speak is not that which will follow your fall
but that which precedes your appearance on the line. . . . You die,
you die before you step onto it. He who dances, dies.

—Jean Genet, *Le funambule*

There are experiences one undergoes but does not talk
about. The experiencing of extreme situations should
be remembered.

Analogies between death and sex are old and after Bataille
became popular, just like the Freudian Eros and Thanatos. I
would like to begin my reflections with sex, because it is, at
least superficially, an easier subject. In our civilization, as opposed to Eastern civilization, sex is much less of a taboo than
death. Death is either embarrassing or terrifying, and while not
many things in our civilization are still taboo, death is.

We all know that there are external and internal experiences,
or, to put it another way, experiences that can be communicated
and those that are memory or knowledge possessed by the
body. To explain an orgasm to someone who has never had one
is impossible. The experience of orgasm is given by the body.

What do we know about sex? Sex can be translated into what is fashionably called "discourse." One can define it using medical, statistical, or pornographical terminology, or with a tone of shared intimate confidences. Yet as discourse, orgasm is different from the body's experience of it. The experience of sex can be described, but it is not the same as the knowledge of that experience. I call it internal knowledge, communicated through the body. This seems significant to me after all those existentialist and phenomenological subtleties thanks to which we have discovered that we can separate ourselves from ourselves and look at ourselves from the outside, that I-am-that-which-thinks-about-itself. On the other hand, there are certain experiences in which the division into "the-I-who-thinks" and "the-I-the-thought" is impossible. This is where the knowledge of the body begins.

After many years pass, as each of us knows, we recall certain sexual experiences. Yet they return to us as memory in our fingertips, as touch, not as discourse. A body remembers another body that has treated it to great physical delight. This is a peculiar memory without names or concepts that functions long after we have forgotten a lover's profile or eye color. Sometimes, years later, when dreaming that we are sleeping with a stranger, we awaken to the bitter taste of guilt on our lips because we feel a spot touched that belonged to another.

An orgasm given by a body is inarticulate speech, a cry, quickened pulse, trembling, sweat. Right now I am trying to change this into discourse, but I know that there is an entire dimension that is inexpressible. Carnal knowledge remains that which is the body, but it is also something more.

We can separate other experiences from ourselves. If my leg hurts, it is as if that leg were a separate part of me. I feel the pain, but I am not the leg that hurts me. I can separate from that part of myself. The profound experiences of sex and death, however, no longer divide the "I" from the "not-I." He whose finger hurts is not only a person "whose finger hurts." He is beyond the finger and its pain. In a sexual act, that division does not exist.

The external and the internal experience are separate: on the one hand the experience that can be communicated on the borderline of discourse (all of literature speaks of love, eroticism, death, etc.), and on the other the experience that we change into discourse but that we know for certain as memory encoded into the body. It is impossible to separate this type of memory from oneself. One can describe only that which can be set apart from oneself.

There is also the following and very basic division into mine and someone else's. For example, one can imagine a pain in the leg as someone else's pain, even though one's own leg hurts. Various acts executed by oneself can be viewed as the action of others: eating, even writing. You are other to yourself: an object. On the other hand, there are experiences where the alienation from the self is impossible. It is then that the *soma* and the *anima* are one. When you can no longer extricate yourself from yourself, the experience is no longer someone else's.

Because of recent events in my life, I have gained an experience that is rare. It is rare to experience dying consciously and then not to die. Strong repressive processes go into action immediately after such an experience. One forgets it or does not want to think about it. It seems to take a certain courage, even *virtu* to think of dying. *Mors interrupta*: The present progressive time.

Because what is death? At the level of discourse, we all know that we will die. I am a man and therefore I must die. Each death, even the most painful, is someone else's, not our own. If we think about our own death then it is as discourse, as an abstraction, or visually, as a movie or video. What is usually allowed us is the fantasy of looking at ourself dead or watching our own funeral. And it is then that our own death is seen as someone else's. The practice of seeing all deaths as someone else's and of thinking about our own death as someone else's hurting leg does not preclude us experiencing a somatic death when we can no longer split apart, where there is no more of that "I die as someone else." No escape into discourse or *imago* is possible in this case. This is *in* me. I cannot separate this from myself.

I have had this experience four times, but most recently the dying lasted quite a long while, and because I knew that this was the fourth infarct, I could not exclude the possibility of its coming to an end. It was then that I came to know not only that I would die but also *how* I would die. I knew I would die in this spasm. I would not be able to separate myself from the dying. I would not be able to say "Jan is dying" the way I said "Jan's leg hurts." Maybe because the pain of an infarct is quite exceptional. Man often loses consciousness when he is suffering from other mortal illnesses, but a heart attack gives one a long period of time to reflect so that one dies in full consciousness.

My first heart attack, four years ago in Poland, was painful. With the second I experienced clinical death. I lost consciousness and it was morning before I saw traces of electric shocks on my chest. I was asked what I remembered. Some people who have returned from clinical death tell of flying away. I remember only a strange sensation, as if someone were piercing the tips of my ears to insert earrings. In the last attack, so painful and long, from about three in the afternoon to four in the morning, I could not separate myself from my body. Just as your skin remembers what sex is, so I now have coded in me what death is, and not as someone else's but as my own. It is difficult to say that this is only a corporeal experience: to divide oneself at such a moment into the body and something that is not the body is impossible. And in that heartrending and piercing pain you know that this is how it is. I am changing the experience into discourse as I have no choice, knowing at the same time that this is possible only to a certain degree. It is coded elsewhere.

I have experienced a lung operation and other operations in my life, and I have always been able to maintain some distance from myself. The anginal pain that is the pain of the heart muscle is such that it is you, it is the very center of your being. In sex and death the ecstasy and pain reach extremes. You as yourself die, but the world also dies with you. I die in something that is not only me. I die in the world. Because the world dies along with me. When you feel a pain that wracks the heart, then everything vanishes together with that pain. There can be no talk of death as relief. There is fear of nonbeing. That is, leaving. In an intense orgasm, there is the same sense of leaving, disappearing, falling away. All this translated into the language of discourse makes it incomprehensible or vague, but the essential moment is when man as a body loses himself, disappears, leaves. Dying is a continuity. Orgasm is a climax: the discontinuity. The French call orgasm "the little death"—"I am dying," the present progressive, uttered by a woman in the throes of orgasm. You melt into something that is not you, into that other person, but that other is, at once, "the other world." In this entanglement you are both whole and the other who is a part of your own flesh. The boundaries of the flesh are obliterated.

In orgasm and death the body is open. It stops being a closed bag of opaque, impenetrable skin. You are embedded in someone's heart as in someone's body. It is turned inside out like a glove. It flows in like sweat and all the fluids of love and death. The heart is not just a sack that pumps blood but one that bears the scars of our loving and our dying until that final day. The heart is both the signified and the signifier, the symbol and its referent. The pump and Eros are one and the same.

In Plato's *Symposium*, Aristophanes' famous half-humorous and half-bitter discourse contains a few amazing discoveries. In the beginning all of us were entwined pairs: man and woman, woman and woman, man and man. These pairs were attached, had four legs, four arms, and two faces. Later they were rent asunder. This is the slapstick side of the tale. Yet not so slapstick, rather tragic, is the notion that these severed bodies long for one another. What is it that longs after itself in this separation? Longing is caused by something that existed earlier. We each know from experience that if one is in love, it seems to be a state imposed from the outside. "I am in love" is a passive condition. Something external has moved us. Usually one says that people were destined or designated or marked for one another. Desire is determined in a split second and is born from a look that reveals the soul and the body. This desire we call Love. Love is given.

But *what* is, what was given? Here I see the profundity of Aristophanes. Couples had once been one but then were cut apart. They seek one another, find each other, or, too, feel a need to see each other again. This was coded in their bodies. In this parable the unconscious knowledge of the body is implied. Bodies were cut apart and then seek each other. But we know that Eros is even deeper than the memory of the flesh.

We use two words in reference to the erotic: sex and love. Throughout the entire Greek and Roman tradition, the word *eros* or *amor* is used and each of these contains both concepts. What is essential is that need, desire, is given free from the outside, it is inborn, a consequence. It is, simultaneously, the need to join bodies and to join souls. I once introduced the concept of soul-bodies or body-souls which desperately seek one another. Which is to say that what is encoded in the body—need and longing—is also the soul. Soul-bodies in Eros are inseparable.

In the experience of death, in the actual experience of dying, you know that you die as a soul-body. I have no doubt about this. When the heart hurts and it hurts very intensely, then the soul-body or body-soul hurts. Maybe that is why the heart is a sign of love. And death—you die alone in the world. You are in love with someone, and lose the very boundaries of your flesh. But you die in something that is not only you, because you die with everything all around. The soul and body are inextricably bound to one another.

"The soul flew from the body," goes a Polish folk song. In my dying the body falls away from the soul. Only the heart, in a great spasm of pain, clings to the soul to the very end.

"When the soul departs from the body," wrote Rabbi Eliezer in the eighth century, "the cry goes forth from one end of the world to the other, but the voice is not heard."

Translated by Lillian Vallee

PART III

GILGAMESH OR MORTALITY

To the memory of Józef Wittlin

I

Two-thirds of him is divine, one-third human." This Sumerian proportion of the divine and the human is very strange. In Greek and Roman mythology there are no gods two-thirds or one-half divine. Divinity is not hereditary as the result of carnal relations between gods and humans. Achilles was not half a god because of his mother, nor was Aeneas although Aphrodite herself was his mother. They had to die as all mortals must. Even Heracles and Dionysus, fathered by Zeus himself, had to die, and a cruel death at that. Being two-thirds divine did not protect Gilgamesh from death either.

"This was the man to whom all things were known; this was the king who knew all the countries of the world. He was wise, he saw mysteries and knew secret things, he brought us a tale of the days before the flood. He went on a long journey, was weary, worn-out with labour, and returning engraved on a stone the whole story." Here is an astounding heroic epic at the very start of which the hero is already worn-out, having engraved his first stone. Can we imagine the first lines of *The Odyssey*: "And he returned to Ithaca weary and worn-out . . ."? Perhaps even the tireless Odysseus grew weary too, but that was much later, after killing the suitors, when he set out on his last journey to the confines of the earth.

The lapis lazuli stone tablet found in the Sumerian tombs or the fired clay brick with the wedge-shaped signs preserved on it is history engraved on stone. The stone and the past recorded on it are one and the same sign. A stone containing a fossilized shell or an imprint of a fern from the Miocene period belongs to natural history and is at the same time its record. There is no great difference between a tablet baked from clay and a pot baked from the same clay. The tablet and the pot are history baked in clay. Just as in Borges's splendid imagination the wall of the city is the library on which the history of the wall is written.

The historical Gilgamesh was king of Uruk and part of the first dynasty of Sumerian kings. But what does being "historical" mean? That a seal was discovered depicting Gilgamesh holding two lions by their tails in his outstretched hands? That on one of the reliefs dating from the eighth century B.C. Gilgamesh is shown with a huge rectangularly trimmed beard holding a small lion as though it were a puppy? Or that on several broken tablets he is referred to as the fifth ruler after the flood and that his reign lasted 126 years? The Babylonian epic dates from after the flood. Like all the epics except the first six chapters of Genesis. The Gilgamesh from after the flood has entered legend and history as the one who enclosed Uruk with walls. "Strong-walled Uruk" was a proverbial saying. Gilgamesh was a great builder.

"Look at it still today; the outer wall where the cornice runs, it shines with the brilliance of copper; and the inner wall, it has no equal. Touch the threshold, it is ancient. Approach Eanna the dwelling of Ishtar, our lady of love and war, the like of which no latter-day king, no man alive can equal. Climb upon the wall of Uruk; walk along it; regard the foundation terrace and examine the masonry: is it not burnt brick and good? The seven sages laid the foundations."

Beyond the walls of Uruk there lies the steppe. Enkidu was conceived in the wilderness. In this civilization of baked brick and of potters, "Enkidu was shaped as in the work of a potter from clay of this earth, like Adam in Genesis out of the *adamah*, nor red clay. Yahweh blew into his nostrils the wind of life." In the Babylonian epic, "Aruru, the goddess of creation conceived an image in her heart, and it was the stuff of Anu of the firmament. She dipped her hands in water and pinched off clay, she let it fall in the wilderness, and noble Enkidu was created." In both epics "man becomes a creature of the flesh."

Conceived in the wilderness Enkidu was a man in the state of nature. He was hairy all over his body; he had long hair like a woman, all in curls like Nisaba, the goddess of grain. "He knew neither people nor homeland," grazed with the gazelles in the hills, ate grass with them, went with the wild animals to the watering hole, and splashed in water with them. But this Sumerian Adam to whom all creatures drew near as to the first man lived on the plains where hunters track and kill animals. A hunter saw Enkidu and grew afraid. Enkidu appeared to him the strongest among the beasts and a messenger of the gods. But this messenger of the gods filled in wolf pits, tore up the traps and snares, set the trapped beasts free. Man in this garden of innocence still belonged to the animal kingdom, but according to the harsh and pitiless anthropology of the first epic, once the plains and wilderness end, the walls of Uruk are already visible. The hunter from the plains went to the king to tell him of the wild man and to lodge a complaint. Gilgamesh sent him back, but with a harlot who sold her body in the temple of Ishtar. "When he sees her, he will come near her. His animals, who grew up in his wilderness, will turn from him."

The epic flow is slow and as in Homer full of repetitions. "After a three days' journey they came to the drinking hole, and there they sat down." The whore and the hunter sat facing and staring at each other without saying a word. They sat like that one day, and then a second day, and on the third day the herds came to the watering hole to drink and Enkidu was with them. Small wild creatures took joy of the water, as did Enkidu, who was born on the plains and grazed with the gazelles. The harlot saw him as he came down from the hills. The hunter said to her: "There he is. Now, woman, make your breasts bare, have no shame, do not delay but welcome his love. Let him see you naked, let him possess your body. When he comes near uncover yourself and lie with him; teach him, the savage man, your woman's art, for when his love is drawn to you the wild beasts that shared his life in the hills will reject him."

For six days and seven nights Enkidu slept with the woman. He had forgotten his animal companions. But when on the seventh day he rose at the break of day and ran to the watering place, the gazelles fled at the sight of him. He wanted to run after them but his knees gave way. "Enkidu was grown weak, for wisdom was in him, and the thoughts of a man were in his heart. So he returned and sat down at the woman's feet, and listened intently to what she said. 'You are wise, Enkidu, and now you have become like a god.' "

In this oldest of *arches,* knowledge is embodied in the sexual act. But in the Babylonian epic the words of the serpent of Eden, "your eyes will be open, and you will be like Gods" (Gen. 3:5), are spoken by a whore.

Now the woman divided her clothing between Enkidu and herself. And they set out on their journey. There is something deeply touching and a kind of wisdom in this expulsion from Paradise in which the wild man and the whore who has covered his nakedness with half of her garments trudge to man's dwellings.

The shepherds set bread before Enkidu. But he did not know how to eat it and could drink only the milk of wild beasts. "Eat bread," said the woman to Enkidu, "it is the staff of life. Drink the wine, it is the custom of the land." Enkidu ate the bread till he was full and drank the wine. His face began to glow and his heart rejoiced. He rubbed his hairy body with olive oil and covered his private parts. Now he belonged to the race of man. He took up arms and tracked the lions so that the shepherds could sleep in peace. And he caught the wolves so that the herds could roam in safety.

Gilgamesh knew of Enkidu. Strange dreams disturbed his sleep. As in the Old Testament, as in Homer and in Greek tragedy, dreams are complicated, indicating hidden fear or unconscious desire. And for that reason, they are prophetic, as are our dreams. Gilgamesh had a dream in which he saw a star fall at his feet. Like a huge stone. He tried to lift it. He could not. It was too heavy. He embraced it as one embraces a woman and hurled it down at his mother's feet. Gilgamesh's mother was Nisun, the goddess of good counsel. Like Achilles and Aeneas, the hero of the Sumerian myth has a protective mother among the cruel or merely indifferent gods. She explained his dream. "The star of heaven is your companion. You tried to lift it; too much for you; you tried to move it; you were not able to move it; you laid him down at my feet so that I compared him with you; like a wife you hugged him."

Nisun knew what she was saying. Gilgamesh was a ruthless tyrant. His desires were boundless. He took the wives of his choicest warriors for himself and stripped brides of their virginity before their husbands. When Enkidu entered the city of Uruk, Gilgamesh at the head of his entourage was on his way to seize a new woman for himself. Enkidu barred his way. The bridal bed had already been prepared.

Enkidu was shorter than Gilgamesh but broader in the shoulders. They started to wrestle. They snorted like two bulls locked in deadly combat. They shattered the gates of the house where the bridal bed stood. They rolled down to the city's wall, which shook. First Enkidu threw Gilgamesh to his knees. Next Enkidu was thrown to the ground. And then "his fury died." There is an unexpected smile in this line. Gilgamesh's face suddenly lighted up. Then Enkidu said: "There is not another like you in the world. Nisun, who is as strong as a wild ox in the byre, she was the mother who bore you."

Gilgamesh and Enkidu embraced and their friendship was sealed.

2

Gilgamesh and Enkidu set out on a solitary expedition to kill the monster Humbaba, who on the orders of the god Enlil guarded the cedar forest in the high mountains, in what is probably modern-day Armenia. When we think of the heroic epic, *The Iliad* comes to mind. Heroic roles and choices are assigned. Or rather preordained. Achilles was given a choice between a long life and everlasting fame. He chose fame. Even the death of his lover, Patroclus, did not shake his resolve. The heroic choices offered to Gilgamesh may appear similar. Enlil, the god of earth and air, decreed Gilgamesh's fate. He sent Gilgamesh a dream. "The meaning of this dream is this. The father of gods has given you kinship, such is your destiny, everlasting life is not your destiny. Because of this do not be sad at heart, do not be grieved or oppressed." In this oldest of epics what is astonishing is not the choice between death and fame, but from the very beginning the presence of fear. Hector, the bravest of the brave, circled three times around the walls of Troy in mortal fear and terror. And perhaps because he experienced fear, he is the most human of all the heroes. But in the entire *Iliad* only Hector knew such fear and had doubts about the value of heroism. Gilgamesh and Enkidu persuade each other to undertake the expedition against the monster; they convince themselves of the heroic necessity, as it were, almost contrary to their own wishes. And they warn each other. From the start the tone of *Gilgamesh* is darker than that of *The Iliad*. The heroic calling is accepted without joy—rather with a seriousness that could be called deadly.

"I have not established my name stamped on brick as my destiny decreed; therefore I will go to the country where the cedar is felled. I will set up my name in the place where the names of famous men are written, and where no man's name is yet written I will raise a monument to the gods. Because of the evil that is in the land, we will go to the forest and destroy the evil; for in the forest lives Humbaba, who is a ferocious giant." But the other voice in this dialogue on heroic necessity is a warning. Even before setting out to the cedar forest, "the eyes of Enkidu were full of tears and his heart was sick." Enkidu was already aware of the monster's power. "He guards the cedar so well that when the wild heifer stirs in in the forest, though she is sixty leagues distant, he hears her. What man would willingly walk into that country and explore its depths? I tell you, weakness overpowers whoever goes near it: it is not an equal struggle when one fights with Humbaba; he is a great warrior, the watchman of the forest never sleeps." In their diggings archaeologists have found Humbaba's head carved in stone from the first half of the first millennium B.C. He has enormous slanted eyes, a flat nose, and a wide-open mouth showing all his teeth in a grin. He is terrifying, but he smiles.

Gilgamesh answered Enkidu: "Where is the man who can clamber to heaven? Only the gods live forever with glorious Shamash, but as for us men, our days are numbered, our occupations are a breath of wind. How is this, already you are afraid! I will go first although I am your lord. . . . Then if I fall I leave behind me a name that endures; men will say of me, 'Gilgamesh has fallen in fight with ferocious Humbaba.' Long after the child has been born in my house, they will say it, and remember."

The axioms and rhetoric of heroism are unchanging and will be repeated in Homer, and a thousand years later in *The Song of Roland*. But the epic of Gilgamesh is unique in that it shows the heroes *before* the test. Death is still a remote word, but already a very tangible fear.

Gilgamesh and Enkidu journeyed for three days before they came to the foot of the mountain covered with the cedar forest. Every evening before the sun set, Gilgamesh dug a small pit in the ground on the nearest hillock and poured into it the choicest grain as an offering to the great Shamash. They slept together in the same bed, tightly embraced, or—the Babylonian epic is sometimes astonishingly precise in its details—when one was asleep the other sat on guard with his chin propped on his knees. "O mountain, dwelling of the gods, send a dream on Enkidu, make him a favourable dream." The mountain sent a dream. But was not a favorable dream. A cold rain drenched him and he drooped like mountain barley. Again they lie down for the night, hold hands, and fall asleep. They sleep united by a common destiny, thrust upon them and at the same time chosen; they sleep united by the necessity for courage and terror. They wake up and tell each other their dreams. Fear enters our lives in dreams. I know those dreams.

Homeric heroes seldom dream. Perhaps because they are seldom alone. Even Odysseus. They seem to be constantly surrounded by companions, friends and enemies, captive women and camp followers; even duels to the death take place with both armies watching. Thus courage and cowardice are displayed before others' eyes, either friendly or hostile. The battles in *The Iliad* always have something of a show about them. On the other hand, Gilgamesh and Enkidu are alone in their expedition against an as yet unvanquished monster. They are alone like the conquerors of mountain peaks joined only by a slender cord. I knew many of them, perhaps the best of my generation. I knew Wawrzyniec, who was radiant and unusually strong in the shoulders, the way Enkidu undoubtedly was. He died in the Alps, buried in an avalanche while on a rescue mission. I knew Moses, with a long black beard like those on the statues of Gilgamesh. He died in the Tatra Mountains while scaling what was for him a relatively easy peak, when an old hook pulled out from the rock. Back then, in the 1940s, everyone tried to economize on equipment. I knew Jacek Poziomka, who blushed and looked like a young girl. He climbed in the Alps all by himself, discovered many new, hitherto untrodden passes, and fell to his death while showing a beginner how to master an overhanging rock. I knew Anna Wichura and Czarny. They all died either in the Tatras—or in Czarny's case, in the Himalayas. Wawrzyniec and Moses would take me along with them on the easier passes and I would keep them company in the lodges. They were not ashamed of their fears and that was the core of their manliness. They would often wake up in the night, sometimes with a scream, and relate their dreams. They were horrifying dreams.

Gilgamesh dreamed that he had a dream but at midnight this second dream let him go and he told his dream to his friend: "Did you call me, or why did I wake? Did you touch me, or why am I terrified? Did not some god pass my, for my limbs are numb with fear? My friend, I saw a third dream and this dream was altogether frightful. The heavens roared and the earth roared again, daylight failed and darkness fell, lightning flashed, fire blazed out, the clouds lowered, they rained down death. Then the brightness departed, the fire went out, and all was turned to ashes."

That last night before entering the cedar forest Gilgamesh dreamed three times and all three dreams were frightful. "I took hold of a wild bull of the wilderness. He bellowed and kicked up earth; dust made the sky dark. I ran for him. With terrible strength he seized my flank. He tore out . . ." Here the lines of the column are worn out, but the next column on the tablet gives an account of yet another dream: "We stood in a deep gorge of the mountain, and suddenly the mountain fell, and beside it we two were like the smallest of swamp flies. Again the mountain fell, it struck me and caught my feet from under me. Then came an intolerable light blazing out, and in it was one whose grace and whose beauty were greater than the beauty of this world. He pulled me out from under the mountain, he gave me water to drink and my heart was comforted." And suddenly, after these illuminations as in the metaphysicians and symbolists many thousand years later, there comes the unexpected: "Friend, let us go down." So said Enkidu the child of the steppe to Gilgamesh, man and two-thirds a god. But they did not go down. At the break of day Gilgamesh took an ax in his hands and together with Enkidu attacked the monster Humbaba, guardian of the cedar forest.

Uruk was surrounded by a barren plain. The expedition to kill the fairy-tale monster must have yet another purpose, although the epic is silent on the subject. Gilgamesh was a legendary builder. And cedar trees are building timber. So after cutting the monster's head off, Gilgamesh proceeded to fell trees and Enkidu dragged them off. Whereupon Enkidu said to Gilgamesh: "Friend, the cedars are felled . . ."

The remaining columns of the fifth tablet are broken.

3

After killing the monster, Gilgamesh returned to Uruk, washed his dirty hair, let it fall over his shoulders, changed into a new robe, and put the royal tiara on his head. Ishtar, the goddess of love and its earthly incarnation, cast her eyes upon him. She instantly fell in love, captivated by his youthful beauty. "Be my bridegroom; grant me the seed of your body." She promised him a house of cedarwood, a chariot of lapis lazuli and gold, the fastest horses, donkeys that could outrun mules, and oxen able to bear any burden. But Gilgamesh rejected Ishtar and her gifts. He showered her with insults. He compared her to a brazier that still smolders, its flame long gone; to a door not tight enough that allows in wind and cold drafts; to pitch that blackens everyone who touches it; to a leaky water bag; to a pinching shoe.

The sexual symbolism of these insults has lost none of its force. But this was not the end of the insults. Gilgamesh reminded Ishtar of her former lovers whom she had discarded, humiliated, or murdered—gods, animals, and men. The first of these was the shepherd and god of regeneration, Dumuzi-Tammuz, sent as a hostage to the underworld. Then she loved the many-colored roller, but she broke his wing, and ever since the roller flies squealing piteously, "Kappi, kappi, my wing, my wing." After this small bird there was a lion; she doted on his tremendous strength, but finally she dug seven pits for him, and when he climbed out of them, she dug another seven pits. She loved a stallion, and then ordained for him the whip, the goad, the halter. She spent many of her nights with a shepherd who baked barley cakes for her and slaughtered baby goats for her; she struck him with a dry stick and turned him into a wolf. She set his own dogs on him. She transformed the gardener of the Edenic garden into a blind mole.

The world of lovers destroyed by this whorish Babylonian Aphrodite is densely populated. Were I to seek parallels to this depiction in Latin literature, I could compare it to accounts in Ovid's *Metamorphoses* in which gods in animal guises and demigods copulate with humans and undergo transformations. But parallels with Greek and to an even greater degree with Latin literature are misleading. The Babylonian gods and goddesses are present in the human world just as they are in the Greek epics and myths, but their interactions and dealings with men are more brutal. The Babylonian gods are more human than their Greek counterparts, but "human" in the worst sense of the word and inscrutable in their actions. Inanna, the Akkadian Ishtar, is more changeable and various than all her later versions and counterparts in the Near East and around the Mediterranean. She is the source of fertility and good crops—hence of copulation for men and beasts—and the renewal of earth when, after the Babylonian rainless season, the rivers are again in full flood, leaving behind the rich, life-giving mud. She is the goddess of lightning and restorative rain. Like Aphrodite-Venus she is both the morning star and the evening star; as the morning star, she awakens men and beasts to their daily toil; as the evening star, she is the guardian of whores and beer taverns. Inanna, the image of all possible contradictions, resembles Demeter, but she is also Persephone, who annually descends into the netherworld.

Even medieval hymns to the Virgin Mary seem almost to repeat the Sumerian litanies to Inanna: "The great queen of heaven, Inanna I will hail! The pure torch that flares in the sky, I will hail! The only one, come forth on high, I will hail." But this mystical Inanna, the light of day, is referred to in the same hymn as "Father Enlil's splendid wild cow."

Of all the divinities, Inanna-Ishtar seems to be the most firmly established in Babylonian ritual, not only on special holidays, when her sacred marriage to the king of Uruk was celebrated, but also in everyday life. The sanctuary, palaces, and gardens of Ishtar occupied one-third of the city; she resided there in her earthly incarnation with her court of virgin priestesses, like the Roman vestals, and courtesan priestesses, who, along with young boys, likewise in the service of the patroness of sacred copulation, offered themselves to pilgrims. It was one such sacred courtesan that Gilgamesh sent to the plains to bring forth Enkidu from the state of nature.

To this day in Naples, in the small towns and villages of southern Italy, in Sicily and Sardinia, one can come upon wayside figures of the Virgin Mary or holy saints adorned with silver votives representing hearts, legs, and eyes that have been miraculously cured by their intercession. But often these same statues have their hands or nose broken off as a punishment for unanswered prayers and offerings. In the insults and abuse that Gilgamesh heaped on Ishtar when she offered herself to him in marriage, we can perhaps detect the same familiar treatment of saints that is still found after thousands of years in the customs and beliefs of the Mediterranean region.

But the contempt of King Gilgamesh for Ishtar, which for those hearing the epic must have been shocking, perhaps even a profanation of the sacred marriage ritual, seems to have yet another, more profound motivation. In the genealogy of the Babylonian gods Ishtar's sister was Ereshkigal, the implacable queen of the underworld. Ishtar herself descends to the kingdom of the dead and sends her first lover there to take her place as a hostage. The symbol and sign of the regeneration of life is at the same time the sign of death. Inanna-Ishtar knows death and is a cause of death: copulation is already tied to death. In Frazer's mythopoetic anthropology the sacred nuptials were the symbolic death of the royal bridegroom. Gilgamesh must have felt divine fear at the prospect of carnal relations with the terrifying Ishtar. But he will pay dearly for his contempt. First, by the death of Enkidu.

Ishtar went to the father of the gods, Anu, and asked him to dispatch to earth the magnificent Bull of Heaven to avenge her and kill Gilgamesh. When Anu tried to resist her demand, Ishtar threatened to open the gates of the underworld and release the dead. The dead outnumber the living; they will eat like the living and devour everything. In both *Gilgamesh* and the Sumerian hymns, this mixture of ordinary experience with the terror of the mythic imagination is astonishing. In all of world literature I do not know of such a simple and obvious statement as that the dead outnumber the living. Were they to be brought back to life, there would be no space or food left for the living.

But the father of gods and men has still other scruples. He reasons like a farmer. The Bull of Heaven will trample on the crops and bring on a drought. For seven years the wheat will produce only seedless husks. The father of the gods asks his cruel daughter if she has stored enough grain for bread and fodder for the cattle. Ishtar was also the symbol of the well-provided storehouse, where, as in the Greek storeroom in Hesiod's *Works and Days,* meat, cheeses, jars of honey, and grain were kept. Her cult was closely linked to the farm economy. Temples served as storehouses.

With a single snort the Bull of Heaven made a hole in the ground and a hundred warriors fell into it. He snorted a second time and swept away two hundred. Then Gilgamesh and Enkidu barred his way. Only a few columns of partially broken lines have survived of this first description of the corrida. Their reading still remains in doubt. First Enkidu seized the Bull of Heaven by the horns. Or—and this reading seems to be more certain—he retreated and approached the bull from the rear and seized him by his thick tail. Then he called out: "Now thrust in your sword between the nape and the horns."

Ritual bull-leaping ceremonies are depicted on the frescoes in the Palace of Knossos on Crete in ochers and reds that have still not faded. The first of the priestesses-acrobats—in necklaces, bracelets, and with a colored cloth around her hips—holds with both hands the left horn of a bull that is charging at her. At this very moment she must leap. Another young female tumbler is shown in the act of making a magnificent *salto mortal,* still almost in the air, legs pointing upward, her hands spread over the bull's back. A third stands behind the bull with upraised arms, as though she were about to seize him by the tail, as Enkidu had. But it is possible that, as in simultaneous representation, the fresco depicts the same girl performing all three positions of a ritual performance.

Even though in the Aegean bull contests no weapons were used and there was no killing, the fresco at Knossos could serve as a splendid illustration for the fight waged by Gilgamesh and Enkidu against the Bull of Heaven. One has the impression that this murderous battle was played out according to the same strict rules as the ballet performed by the female tumblers. The frescoes in the Palace of Knossos date from about the middle of the second millennium B.C. At almost the same period that the Old Babylonian version of *Gilgamesh* was written in the Akkadian language.

After killing the Bull of Heaven, Gilgamesh and Enkidu split open its flank and cut out its heart and offered it to the sun god, Shamash. Then Ishtar, disguised as a mourner, mounted the walls of Uruk. Upon seeing her, Enkidu tore off the bull's right thigh and threw it in her face: "If I could reach you . . . I'd hang his guts around your arm!"

Even today in Andalusian corridas the matador has the right to cut off the ears and sometimes the tail of the bull he has killed as the reward for his splendid performance. White-powdered women in black mantillas looking as though they had stepped from a painting by Goya watch the killing of the bull, their cheeks blushing from excitement, their eyes sparkling as in the act of love. The matador has the privilege of offering the bull's ears to the senorita of his choice. The bull contests in Sumer, as later on Crete and on the Iberian Peninsula today, must have been not only a show performance but also a rigorous ceremony full of symbolic meanings like a religious ritual. Throwing a hunk of the bull's meat at Ishtar, the goddess of copulation, must have been not only an insult but a symbolic sexual humiliation as well.

Now the stage is swarming with multitudes of people as in a Persian miniature. High above, on a terrace of the highest of the walls, Ishtar, surrounded by her male and female slaves of love, harpists, lutenists, and singers, intones a lament over the remains of the Bull of Heaven. Down below, Gilgamesh and his choicest goldsmiths weigh the bull's horns. They were thirty pounds each and plated with lapis lazuli two fingers thick.

Festivities and celebrations are taking place on all the city's squares and in the courtyard of the royal palace. It was only late at night that Enkidu and Gilgamesh lay down to sleep. And as happened on the last night in the mountains on their expedition to the cedar forest, Enkidu suddenly woke up with a start: "Ah, such a dream I had. . . . All the gods sat in council."

In Sumerian myths when the gods gather for a council it is a bad omen for humans. For killing Humbaba and the Bull of Heaven, either Gilgamesh or Enkidu had to die. Enlil, the god of earth, chose Enkidu. In vain did Shamash testify that Enkidu was innocent: the killing of the monster Humbaba was done at his command and with his help. The sun god failed to convince the angry god of earth. In the epic of Gilgamesh, calling into question the justness of the verdict given at the council of the gods is very human and humanely touching. The Sumerians knew that death is inevitable and that it is in vain to ask why. "And the time comes"—according to one of the oldest Babylonian texts—"for the umbilical cord to be cut and there is no answer other than silence." Enkidu must die; guilty or not. And from that point on to the end of the epic all will be somber.

4

In the first chapter of *Mimesis,* which after almost half a century is still one of the most brilliant examples of the sort of literary criticism that explores the ever-changing image of man, Erich Auerbach contrasts the Homeric world, always uniformly bathed in light, to the Old Testament narratives and their constant transitions from light to darkness. In the Greek epic the heroes, and the world in which they live, are shown in relief as on a frieze, but the picture lacks depth. In the biblical epic, as in Rembrandt's portraits and on his large canvases, daylight or the glare of torches is focused on a single point—on the hands or the face of the protagonist of the drama—and the rest of the world is drowned in darkness. The Homeric heroes, their armor, their horses, their ships, and their tents are always displayed in the foreground and carry with them "the present [which] fills both the stage and the reader's mind completely." Unchangeable, untroubled (Hector being the only possible exception), untouched by either time or events, they "wake every morning as if it were the first day of their lives." After two decades, Odysseus returns to Ithaca as if he had been gone for a single night. Helen is no more disturbed by pangs of conscience than her smooth cheeks have been marked by wrinkles.

But Abraham, Jacob, and David are torn by doubts; they are unfathomable to themselves, just as the world is unfathomable to them. And God is unfathomable, too, as are his judgments. For a brief moment they came out from behind the "shadow line" into the dazzling brightness, which they will never fully understand and will never forget, but even before dusk falls they sink back again into the "shadow line."

The narrative of the first six of the twelve tablets of the epic of Gilgamesh seems to belong to the Homeric type, but it abruptly changes with the death of Enkidu and takes on the characteristics of the biblical story. For Auerbach, the Old Testament stories are, in comparison with the Homeric legend, to a much higher degree a universal drama. *Gilgamesh,* the oldest of the epics, has not ceased to be a universal drama after almost five thousand years, perhaps because its major theme is death. Or rather dying.

The representations of death in world literature are many. But I do not know of an image of *dying* as moving as that of

Enkidu. Dying, which contrary to appearances is not at all a common experience, is given, but not to everyone, as one's *own* dying—when we are ready to accept it or to accompany someone else's dying. Fate is our own double, but as Hegel has pointed out, it is "our double perceived as the enemy within." In the act of dying, as we achieve awareness that death is inevitable, final, and without hope, our own life seems *alien,* since it can be taken away from us and we tend to suspect that from the very start there must have been an error. If only we could start all over again, everything would be different and we would not have to die at all. Proust knew about that.

When Enkidu realizes that he must die, he curses both the sacred harlot and the hunter who brought her to the wilderness so that she could lead him out of the state of nature. Adam, expelled from the garden of Eden, his nakedness covered, curses Eve on whose account he must die: "Listen, woman. I will decree your fate, a destiny that will have no end and will last forever. I will curse you with a great curse. . . . You shall never enter the tavern of young women; the road will be your dwelling place . . . the shadow of the wall will be your resting place." To anyone who knew the stifling heat of the Near East, the last curse must have sounded especially cruel. And the Babylonian curse does not end there. "The dust of the potter's crossroad will be your dwelling place. The desert will be your bed. Thorn and bramble will skin your feet, the besotted and the thirsty will hit your face." God curses Adam in similar fashion: "Thorns and thistles it shall bring to you; and you shall eat the plants of the field" (Gen. 3:18).

But at just this point the voice of the sun god Shamash was heard on high: "Why, Enkidu, do you curse the love-priestess, the woman who would feed you with the food of the gods, and would have you drink wine that is the drink of kings, and would clothe you in a great garment, and would give you beautiful Gilgamesh as a companion?" Shamash, speaking from the

heavens, represents wisdom, both divine and human, according
to which Enkidu had no cause to complain of his fate. But what
is the use of this wisdom in the face of death? Enkidu has to die,
now! *He* has to, not someone else. In this oldest epic we find
deeply moving this opposition or rather this *coexistence* of the
world's reasons and the dying man's reasons present in the dialogue between god and man.

In *Gilgamesh* existential dread—the conscious and the unconscious—which *I* am for *myself,* is most often portrayed in
dreams. "Friend, I saw a dream in the night. There was a man,
his face was dark. The paws of a lion were his paws; the talons
of an eagle were his talons. He grabbed a tuft of my hair . . .
and led me down to the house of darkness, the house where one
goes in never comes out again, the road that, if one takes it, one
never comes back, the house that, if one lives there, one never
sees light, the place where they live on dust, their food is mud."
And there follows what is perhaps the most startling image in
this Sumerian Hades: "Their clothes are like birds' clothes, a
garment of wings, and they see no light, living in blackness."

Enkidu visits the underworld, as did Odysseus and then
Aeneas. But he is taken there in this dream before death as
though he were already one of the dead. "Ereshkigal, the queen
of the underworld, lifting her head looked directly at me—*me:*
'Who has brought this one here . . .?' "

Dying is a long process. Sometimes for others, but more
often for oneself. Enkidu dies a long death both for himself for
Gilgamesh. On the day that the dream came to him, Enkidu lay
down, stricken with a sudden illness: "A second day Enkidu is
lying on his bed; a third day and a fourth day, Enkidu on his
bed; a fifth, a six, a seventh, an eighth, a ninth and a tenth day
Enkidu lies sick. . . . An eleventh and a twelfth day." Dying is
monotonous. And perhaps only the simplest counting of days
can convey the monotony of dying.

Gilgamesh stays with Enkidu to the very end as he goes about dying. "Now what is this sleep that has taken hold of you? You've become dark. You can't hear me. I touched your heart, it does not beat." Then Gilgamesh covered his friend's face with a veil the way one covers the face of one's wife. For six days and seven nights Gilgamesh kept vigil by his friend's corpse until he saw a worm crawling slowly out of Enkidu's nose. This bitter knowledge offers no illusions or consolations; death means the decay of the body and the repulsive physicality of the body's decay is shown in all its horror.

Gilgamesh placed Enkidu's body in the royal tomb and ordered his statue to be sculpted in gold and plated in lapis lazuli. All of Uruk had to go into mourning for him. Warriors and whores participated in the lamentations. But all that was simply part of the official ceremony. On the profound existential level of the epic, Gilgamesh's grief stemmed from his identification with Enkidu: "I have been to you your mother, and your father; I will weep for you in the wilderness." Images of the half-savage Enkidu roaming the plains reappear in this shocking depiction of death, which belongs to the order of nature. "Your mother was a gazelle, and . . . your father who created you, a wild ass. You were raised by creatures with tails, and by the animals of the wilderness, with all its breadth."

Enkidu was conceived in the wilderness in order to be Gilgamesh's double. But the doubleness reveals its hidden meaning only when Enkidu is dying. This doubleness lies not in their strength or heroic prowess or in their manly love but in the fact that they are both mortal. The ultimate identity lies in death. Gilgamesh wept bitterly for his friend Enkidu: "Me! Will I too not die like Enkidu?"

Gilgamesh identifies with Enkidu, but with the Enkidu who lived on the plains. Covered with long hair that he neglected to trim, in a lion's hide, he roamed the wilderness. "Sorrow has come into my belly. I fear death. I will seize the

road to the house of Utnapishtim." Utnapishtim, like the biblical Noah, was saved from the flood in an ark he had built. But
in contrast to the book of Genesis, in the Babylonian epic written in cuneiform one thousand years earlier, the gods conferred
the gift of immortality on Utnapishtim and his wife and they
live forever at the limits of the world.

5

Gilgamesh's journey was a lengthy one. No mortal had
ever ventured so far. He finally came to the mountains at the
ends of the earth, which support the heavens and serve as the
gate through which the sun rises and sets. The gate is guarded
by two giant male and female scorpions. Then Gilgamesh went
through the tunnel of darkness to the other end of the earth,
where the gods have their garden. As in the Garden of Eden of
the most ancient Hebrew tradition ("A river flowed out of
Eden to water the garden . . . where there is gold, and the gold
of that land is good; bdellium and onyx stone are there" (Gen.
2:10–12), and in the garden of the Arabic tradition, where the
trees flower and bear fruit in the form of the most precious
stones: sapphire, lapis lazuli, and rubies. Gilgamesh's journey is
the first in a series of fantastic and wondrous expeditions, and
we can perhaps find a distant echo of it in the medieval quest
for the Holy Grail. But in contrast to the many journeys under-
taken in the thousands and thousands of years that followed,
Gilgamesh goes on his travels alone and in a state of despair. He
is sick and the name of his malady is death.

At the other end of the earth, amid the vineyards she culti-
vates, is a tavern kept by the beautiful Siduri. If we think of the
Odyssey, she could be compared to the beautiful nymph
Kalypso. But perhaps this beautiful veiled barmaid who sits
among the golden bowls and plates is yet another incarnation of
Ishtar, who was the patroness of taverns and tavern keepers.

Ishtar fell in love with Gilgamesh when he stood before her as beautiful as a god after killing the monster Humbaba. The Gilgamesh who now stood at the gate of the tavern is covered with the skins of wild animals, his hair is matted and his cheeks sunken. A ravaged Gilgamesh stood before Ishtar transformed into the keeper of a tavern. Ravaged by his long wanderings, but destroyed even more by the fear of death that had never left him for a moment. "How can I keep still? How can I be silent? The friend I loved has turned to clay. Me, shall I not lie down like him, never again to move?"

Ishtar, the tavern keeper residing among the jugs of wine and golden bowls, answers the mortal who seeks immortality: "Gilgamesh, where are you hurrying to? You will never find that life for which you are looking. When the gods created man they allotted to him death, but life they retained in their own keeping. As for you, fill your belly with good things; day and night, night and day, feast and rejoice. Let your clothes be fresh, bathe yourself in water, cherish the little child that holds your hand, and make your wife happy in your embrace; for this too is the lot of man."

This is sound advice given by a wise woman. But neither a woman's advice, nor earlier the divine advice of the sun god Shamash, is of any use to one who knows that he must die. The living cannot console the dying. And there can be no comfort from the heavens. In the tragic undercurrent that increasingly dominates *Gilgamesh,* dying is the *unhuman* human condition. All that Gilgamesh wants from the beautiful barkeeper with her golden bowls is for her to show him the way to the immortal Utnapishtim, who is called the Remote.

The Babylonians imagined the earth as a flat disk covered by the cupola of the sky as by a bell jar, under which the gods dwell. On all sides, the plate of the earth is surrounded by the ocean. Beyond the vast expanse of water, with which even simple contact means death, is the dwelling place of the Remote and his wife saved from the flood. In the epic of *Gilgamesh,* the prototype of all myths, the Sumerian Charon, the boatman who ferries the dead across the sea of death, is called Urshanabi.

The story of the flood told to Gilgamesh seemingly has no connection with the main theme of the epic and perhaps was added at some later point, in an altered version. But unlike the biblical flood, which was a punishment for making the wickedness of men great in the earth as the result of copulation between the fallen angels and the daughters of men, the Babylonian flood in *Gilgamesh* had no motivation or cause. The same god Enlil—who had flown into a rage on learning that Utnapishtim had been warned of the coming flood, built an ark, and saved his life—later confers immortality on him. The Babylonian gods are capricious and their deeds and discriminations between good and evil are inscrutable to human beings. They are blind and deaf to our fate. As William Moran, one of the subtlest commentators on *Gilgamesh,* points out, "The story of the Flood can be seen as a paradigm of man's fate."

> You can see how little compassion the Gods
> have shown in all that's happened; they
> who are called our fathers, who begot us,
> can look upon such suffering.
> No one can foresee what is to come.
> What is here *now* is pitiful for us.
> (Sophocles, *The Women of Trachis*)

The Sophoclean tragic vision can be discerned in *Gilgamesh.* Utnapishtim, who survived the flood, has discovered the great indifference of the gods. He knows that all that is human and earthly must pass. "Do we build a house forever? Do we seal a contract for all time? Does the river forever rise higher, bringing on floods? Does the dragonfly leave its husk . . . the face that looks at the face of Shamash? From the beginning there is no permanence. The sleeping and the dead, how like brothers they are! Do they not both make a picture of death?"

"In your case, now," said Utnapishtim to Gilgamesh, "who will assemble the gods for you so that the life you seek you may discover? Test yourself! Don't sleep for six days and seven nights." But scarcely had Gilgamesh lain down on the bedding when sleep enveloped him like soft wool that unwinds imperceptibly from the skein. For six days and seven nights Enkidu slept with the priestess of Ishtar, who with an art known to all women made him an equal to the gods. For six days and seven nights Gilgamesh sat at the bedside of the dead Enkidu. The Babylonian flood lasted six days and seven nights; its origin, ending, and meaning remained inscrutable to humans. Six days and seven nights Gilgamesh slept in the house of the immortal one. Six days and seven nights is the symbolic time of transformations—a *rite de passage*. It is the time needed for the creation of the world. "And on the seventh day God finished his work which he had done, and he rested on the seventh day" (Gen. 2:2).

When Gilgamesh woke up, it seemed to him that he had slept for only a moment. But Utnapishtim's wife baked bread every night and put the freshly baked loaf by the bedside of the sleeping Gilgamesh to mark the irrevocable passage of time. Gilgamesh woke up among seven loaves of bread, the first dried out, the second leathery, the third soggy, the fourth molded, the fifth mildewed, the sixth rotten, only the seventh still hot. And then Gilgamesh understood that sleep is not only the likeness but also the antechamber of death. Such self-knowledge contains elements of Ovid's *dormiens cadaver* from the *Metamorphoses*. Man is a corpse who is *still* asleep.

> "What can I do? Where can I go?
> A thief has stolen my flesh.
> Death lives in the house where my bed is,
> and wherever I set my feet, there Death is."

All that remains for Utnapishtim to do is to send Gilgamesh back. But first he will send for the boatman, Urshanabi, and tell him to take Gilgamesh to the washing place, where he is to wash off the dirt and dust of his wanderings and put on his clean, naked body the ceremonial robe offered him. It is astonishing how many times the hero bathes in this oldest and shortest of epics in which the mythic and the marvelous are interwoven in the same fabric with a faithful picture of customs and basic human experience.

When Gilgamesh and the boatman came back from the washing place to say farewell, Utnapishtim's wife pleaded for one more gift for that stubborn wanderer through the waters of death. "I shall reveal a secret thing," said Utnapishtim, "it is a mystery of the gods that I am telling you. There is a plant that grows under the water, it has a prickle like a thorn, like a rose; it will wound your hands, but if you succeed in taking it, then your hands will hold that which restores his lost youth to a man." Gilgamesh sailed on the sea, tied heavy stones to his feet, and went down to the very bottom. He pulled up the plant, cut loose the stones, and let the current carry him up and cast him ashore. "I will take it to Uruk of the strong walls," said Gilgamesh to the boatman, Urshanabi, "there I will give it to the old men to eat. Its name shall be 'The Old Men Are Young Again'; and at last I shall eat it myself and have back all my lost youth."

They sailed back for twenty double hours before they broke their fast. Then they continued for thirty double hours more before they saw a pool of clear, cool water. Gilgamesh took off his robe in order to refresh himself in the water. Meanwhile, a snake noiselessly darted forth, snatched the plant, and devoured it, casting off its old skin onto the sand.

When God expelled Adam and Eve from the Garden of Eden, he clothed them first to cover their nakedness in "garments of skins" (Gen. 3:21). What kind of skins? In the Garden of Eden even the animals did not know death. According to the old rabbinical tradition, it was the skin cast off by a snake. Once again, it seems, we can find the prototype of the biblical myth in *Gilgamesh*. The serpent "more subtle than any other creature" (Gen. 3:1) who tempted Eve, thus causing mankind from then on to be subject to death, had also stolen from Gilgamesh the plant that "restores his lost youth to a man."

Gilgamesh sat in the sand and wept bitterly. Perhaps only then did he understand the teaching of the Babylonian Noah that everything human is given over to destruction. On the twelfth and final tablet of the Akkadian version of the epic of Gilgamesh the last column is completely destroyed, with the exception of only one sentence: "He who saw everything . . ."

Gilgamesh and Urshanabi abandoned the boat and proceeded on foot. Once again twenty double hours passed before they ate their first meal. After an additional thirty double hours they stopped to rest. When they finally arrived at the gates of Uruk, Gilgamesh said to the faithful boatman: "Go up, Urshanabi, onto the walls of Uruk. Inspect the base, view the brickwork. Is not the very core made of oven-fired brick? Did not the seven sages lay down its foundations?"

In a true epic the beginning is an ending and the ending is a repetition of the beginning. The epic of Gilgamesh begins and ends with praise of the walls of Uruk, which alone of things made by man seem able to defy the destruction of time.

6

The road from Tunis to Carthage goes toward the sea through suburbs with modern white villas among palm trees and flowers. Only occasionally at the intersections are there stone tombs of Moslem saints, the marabouts, tombs crowned with a white dome, invariably onion shaped, the sharp end pointing into the cloudless sky. Closer to the sea the houses become less numerous, and through the palm trees there can be seen more and more frequently ribbons of sand in the two colors with which Tunis is forever associated in our memory—yellow and a red changing from light pink to an almost flaming red.

The plateau, from which one can see the old port on one side and the ruins of the Roman amphitheater on the other, is an enormous empty square. Little boys stopped playing ball for a moment and tried to sell us Greek and Roman coins and olive-oil lamps, which, of course, had just been taken out of the kiln. "Where is Carthage," I asked. Our guide raised his index finger, then pointed straight down. "Under us," he said.

Carthage was conquered by the Roman legions in the Third Punic War. The siege lasted two years and is regarded in the history of the wars of the period as one of the fiercest. And the defense of the city was one of the most heroic. The women cut off their hair to make rope for stone-throwing machines. The children heated the cauldrons from which scalding water was poured on the assailants below.

After the city had been taken, the ruins burned for six days and seven nights. Then Carthage was leveled and the ground sown with salt so that nothing would grow there. *Carthago delenda est.* But that was not the end of Carthage. Scipio Aemilianus, the son of Scipio Africanus, once again covered over the ruins and had the forum for a new Roman city built on them. Five centuries later it was destroyed by the Vandals.

What now remains of the ancient city of Carthage are the outlines of the foundations of the Punic houses that archaeologists have only recently excavated under the successive layers containing the ruins of Roman houses. In the sanctuaries have been discovered tomb steles, several rings, bracelets, and necklaces as well as strange tiny masks representing demons, all now housed in two small rooms at the Bardo Museum in Tunis. But the most interesting are three or four stone statues representing most probably a priest, his eyes wide open and always making the same gesture. He keeps his left arm resting on his breast, while his right arm is bent at the elbow, the palm open and fingers held together, reaching to the level of his shoulder. We can easily interpret this gesture. It is a sign to stop the intruder who has entered a holy place.

Carthage was destroyed almost two thousand years after the destruction of Uruk and Ur.

O thou shrine of Nippur, a bitter lament set up thy lament.
O thou brickwork of the Ekur, a bitter lament set up thy lament.
O thou brickwork of the Urukug, a bitter lament set up thy lament.
O thou shrine Egmalah, a bitter lament set up thy lament.
O thou city of *name*, thou has been destroyed.

Ur and Uruk were then destroyed for the first but not the last time. As Jeremiah prophesied: "The sea has come up to Babylon; she is covered with its tumultuous waves. Her cities become a horror, a land of drought and desert, a land in which no one dwells, and through which no son of man passes" (51:42–43).

Note

Quotations from the epic of *Gilgamesh* come from the following English translations: John Gardner and John Maier, *Gilgamesh Translated from the Sin-Leqi-Unninni Version* (New York, 1984); N. K. Sandars, *The Epic of Gilgamesh* (Baltimore, 1964); A. Hediel, *The Gilgamesh Epic and Old Testament Parallels* (Chicago, 1949). Other texts used: "Hymn to Inanna," in Thorkild Jacobsen, *The Treasures of Darkness* (New Haven, Conn., 1969); Michael Jameson, trans., *The Women of Trachis by Sophocles* (Chicago, 1984); S. Kramer, trans., *Lamentation over the Destruction of Ur,* The Oriental Institute Assyriological Studies, no. 12 (Chicago, 1940).

Translated by Jadwiga Kosicka

Index